W9-BTZ-911

MAR 1 4 2020

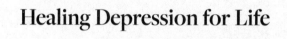

Healing Depression for Life

The
Personalized
Approach
that Offers New
Hope for
Lasting Relief

GREGORY L. JANTZ, PhD
WITH KEITH WALL

Healing
Depression
for Life

TYNDALE
MOMENTUM®

The nonfiction imprint of
Tyndale House Publishers, Inc.

Visit Tyndale online at www.tyndale.com.

Visit Tyndale Momentum online at www.tyndalemomentum.com.

TYNDALE, *Tyndale Momentum*, and Tyndale's quill logo are registered trademarks of Tyndale House Publishers, Inc. The Tyndale Momentum logo is a trademark of Tyndale House Publishers, Inc. Tyndale Momentum is the nonfiction imprint of Tyndale House Publishers, Inc., Carol Stream, Illinois.

Healing Depression for Life: The Personalized Approach that Offers New Hope for Lasting Relief

Copyright © 2019 by Dr. Gregory Jantz. All rights reserved.

Cover illustration by Jennifer Phelps. Copyright © Tyndale House Publishers, Inc. All rights reserved.

Author photograph by Karen Obrist, copyright © 2014. All rights reserved.

Designed by Jennifer Phelps

Edited by Jonathan Schindler

Published in association with The Bindery Agency, www.TheBinderyAgency.com.

All Scripture quotations, unless otherwise indicated, are taken from the Holy Bible, *New International Version*,® *NIV*.® Copyright © 1973, 1978, 1984, 2011 by Biblica, Inc.® Used by permission. All rights reserved worldwide.

Scripture quotations marked NLT are taken from the *Holy Bible*, New Living Translation, copyright © 1996, 2004, 2015 by Tyndale House Foundation. Used by permission of Tyndale House Publishers, Inc., Carol Stream, Illinois 60188. All rights reserved.

For information about special discounts for bulk purchases, please contact Tyndale House Publishers at csresponse@tyndale.com, or call 1-800-323-9400.

ISBN 978-1-4964-3461-6

Printed in the United States of America

25 24 23 22 21 20 19
7   6   5   4   3   2   1

RO456905341

This book is dedicated to the scores of people
I've known who had the courage to confront
their depression . . . and found healing.

Contents

Foreword

Throughout my life, I've battled depression. During my childhood, it came as a dark veil, accompanied by traumatic childhood experiences and carried through my blood and brain by what we now call "depression genetics."

Because of my moods, when I was ten years old, my parents took me to a psychiatrist. I got some help but also found more trauma, in the form of sexual molestation. This experience led to still more depression.

Both the already-established depression and the molestation would later become two pillars of my adult resilience. But a boy could not know that then. I only knew confusion, pain, and tunnels of darkness. As the trauma and darkness moved through my adolescence, I went back into therapy at sixteen, a boy-man who spent the next ten years talking, journaling, medicating, self-medicating, writing, thinking, feeling, withdrawing, competing, risking, and loving my way out.

Each process worked for its part, and ten years of therapy helped a great deal. By my early thirties, I authentically felt that I was an adult who had been healed of childhood trauma and was quite functional, quite alive. But I still battled depression. Medication helped, as did getting better sleep, ending addictions, eating no more junk or food I was allergic to, exercising, forming close relationships, growing in self-awareness, and engaging in therapy, spiritual practices, and discipline. Indeed, many of the practices represented in the chapters of this new book by Dr. Gregory Jantz became best practices in my own life.

But depression is a song inside us, and it keeps singing. We need constant help, constant companionship, and constant self-awareness.

And we need good teachers.

Gregg Jantz is a good teacher. *Healing Depression for Life* is a constant and powerful companion. I can attest to its best practices in the way that someone who stares at dawn skies for months can attest to seeing only little sun or no sun at all—just a dullness, a numb, inhibited destiny of narrowed corners. But then something pivots, the world moves, the person moves, and the person has the new feeling of seeing full on—without opaqueness, without fear, without an internal storm—the lovely world again. Healing depression for life is a real concept, even though we know it gets its greatest power from our individual ability to live it out as a prolific metaphor.

Meeting Dr. Gregg Jantz, talking with him about depression and addiction, and providing consulting and training to the clinic he founded—The Center: A Place of Hope—has been one of the highlights of my career. We've worked together on projects not just in Edmonds, Washington, where the clinics are nestled at the base of beautiful hills and mountains, but elsewhere in the country too—speaking, training, researching, and writing together.

Gregg and his team live at the leading edge of whole-person health and wellness. They take on the big issues, the big themes, and the epic journeys of sadness, addiction, anxiety, pain, and loss, and they do so with best practices always in mind. The clinic, its practitioners, and Dr. Jantz give new hope to their clients. Throughout my friendship with Dr. Jantz and my consulting work with The

Center, I've most admired two basic precepts of the work, both of which ground this book:

- the importance of spiritual process (connectedness, mystery, purpose, mindfulness), which provides a basis for healing depression
- the idea that mind and body cannot be separated in a human soul and person: to heal depression, we must heal the body, too

A pill might be helpful for a person, but a pill is not enough for either of these precepts to be fully realized. The body requires action, as does the mind, in the same way a pilot is only as good as the airplane he or she is managing.

In *Healing Depression for Life*, a lifetime of Dr. Jantz's own work joins a lifetime of confidential client stories and the assistance of his colleagues and science-based research to form an impressive, accessible, gently written, and essential book for those on the path of depression.

No matter where you are in your journey—whether you are currently struggling with depression or one of your progeny or family members is haunted by the darkness—you will find in this book a blueprint for a healing process that will provide you with what you need to succeed in the struggle.

With depression statistics skyrocketing today, The Center's approach is not just timely; it can also be life saving.

Dr. *Michael Gurian*
New York Times *bestselling author*
of Saving Our Sons *and*
The Minds of Girls

Help Is on the Way

*If Depression Has You Feeling Hopeless,
You've Come to the Right Place*

Depression is a worn-out word these days. Sports fans are "depressed" after their teams lose. Most news reporting is criticized for being "depressing." The blogosphere and social media sites are clogged with every viewpoint under the sun as to the causes and cures of depression. As happens with most overused words, the real meaning of this one is fast becoming vague and abstract to many people.

But not to the millions of Americans who suffer from its all-too-real effects every year.

And not to me. As a mental health expert, I resist assigning the word *depression* to others as an impersonal diagnosis with professional detachment or superiority. Over the years, I've learned an enormous amount about the medical science of this condition. But by far the lessons I value most are those I learned from the inside out. I understand firsthand how deep the cavern of depression can go and how dark it can get—because I've been there.

I know how it feels to wake up in the morning and wonder where I'll find the energy to take my next breath.

I have looked out at the once-vibrant world and seen only shades of gray, dull and flattened.

I have felt the desperate and terrifying impulse to run away from my life, as fast and as far as my legs would carry me.

If you recognize these feelings in yourself because you've experienced them too, you needn't worry that the book in your hands is just another list of smug or simplistic "solutions" or half-baked theories that don't bear much resemblance to your own experience. If you suffer from depression, you know very well that the answers you seek aren't easy or simple—or you would have found them already. You know better than anyone that you face an entrenched enemy, devious and determined and able to attack from many angles and in many forms.

But what you may not know is . . . *that's not the end of the story*.

None of us is truly stuck in that dark place with no hope of return. I wrote this book because I'm excited to help you see this for yourself. I want to share with you the single most important thing I've ever learned about depression—priceless knowledge gained in the trenches of personal struggle. It is simply this:

Depression does not need to be a life sentence.

You *can* heal.

How can I be so sure? Because recent findings in the study of depression have yielded new and effective treatments. Because I've witnessed healing happen in case after case of treatment-resistant depression at my clinic. And because I've experienced healing in my own life too.

Wounded Healer

In the early 1980s, I had already launched The Center: A Place of Hope, a Seattle-area clinic specializing in treating depression, anxiety, eating disorders, and other significant mental health issues. The effectiveness of our work with those who were struggling with eating disorders had drawn broad attention, and my team and I had begun to develop the "whole person" model for helping people heal after other methods had fallen short. As we refined and revised this approach, we discovered that our clients achieved substantial progress with our direction and their hard work. More and more desperate individuals came to our clinic; media opportunities became frequent; speaking engagements and consultations crowded my calendar. I was busy advising others on how to take charge of their overall health and lifestyle habits to achieve the change they so badly wanted in their lives and was seeing real, tangible results.

All the while, my own life was rapidly falling apart.

Working six days a week at a grueling (and foolish) pace, I had begun to make the classic mistake of not practicing what I preached. My diet was a wreck, and I made no attempt to exercise. I self-medicated with false comforts like junk food, excessive caffeine, and other unhealthy choices. Nighttime became a nightmare of insomnia and crippling anxiety. Days were not much better. A deep emotional apathy and physical lethargy overtook my waking hours. I gained weight and looked haggard. Not surprisingly, my spiritual life was coming unglued as well. For decades my Christian faith had been a source of joy and guidance, but now it felt like an obligation, another set of to-do items on my endless checklist. Depleted and desperate, I was not much better off than many of my patients.

In spite of continued success in my psychology practice (a miracle in itself), I began to fear I'd chosen the wrong vocation, going so far as to plan my escape to a whole new city. I chose Colorado Springs—far away from our home in coastal Washington—for no other reason than my family had vacationed there when I was a child, so it somehow felt safe, an oasis amid chaos. Truth be told, I felt lost. My depression was so deep I was willing to walk away from everything I had worked hard to build and upon which my family depended.

After months of this downward spiral, something happened that turned my life around—without which I honestly don't know where I'd be today.

My lifeline came, ironically enough, in the form of total exhaustion. The people who cared about me most—family members and close friends—stepped in and stepped up to steer me back on course, demonstrating equal measures of loving support and tough love. They worked to put me on a rigidly controlled daily routine that reinstated the healthy habits I knew but wasn't practicing. This involved shortened workdays, regular walks, improved sleep habits, a nutritious diet, time for prayer and reflection, and much more. I had to set new boundaries, and I committed to staying within them, and so I began my long climb back to health and well-being. Throughout that hard and daunting process, I became sold on the whole-person treatment philosophy that has guided our work at The Center for many years now.

I also gained the confidence that allows me to say to you today, *you can heal too.*

Something's Amiss

In 2016, more than 16 million Americans (6.7 percent of all US adults) experienced at least one major depressive episode. And yet, though the typical modern treatment approach for depression has existed for more than fifty years, the number of people suffering from the disorder just keeps climbing. Research studies report that incidents of diagnosed depression are higher than ever.[1] Furthermore, the current popular treatment choices fail to help as many as one-third of all depression patients, who derive little or no benefit from medications or psychotherapy. Millions more experience some relief through these methods but continue to relapse into minor or major depression throughout their lives. Why is lasting freedom from depression so hard to come by? It's a perplexing and exasperating question.

Fortunately, more than thirty years of practice and experience at The Center have led us to some compelling conclusions—all of which will be discussed in detail in the chapters ahead. The nation is losing ground in its battle with depression, due in part to one or more of the following:

Over-prescription and misuse of medication. In The Center's early years, we saw clients who had tried or were currently taking no more than two or three medications. These days, our average incoming client is taking five different medications or more. Often these drugs contribute to the problem or create new issues. More troubling, these multiple medications sometimes compete dangerously with each other in the patient's body or combine in unpredictable ways. And that's before accounting for side effects the pharmaceutical companies have already identified.

In fact, a recent study found that one-third of adults in the US may be unknowingly using prescription drugs that could cause depression or increase the risk of suicide. As one report stated, "A team of scientists at the University of Illinois at Chicago warned that over 200 commonly prescribed drugs carry warnings that depression or suicide are potential side effects. But patients and clinicians may be unaware of this link because the drugs may treat conditions unrelated to depression or mental health. Those include some painkillers; blood pressure and heart medication; hormonal birth control pills; proton pump inhibitors; and antacids."[2] Indeed, many medications can lead to serious physical symptoms, which are often treated with—you guessed it—more medication!

Relying completely on medication as the solution. When general practitioners prescribe psychotropic medications without the input of a psychiatrist or other mental health specialist, and when patients request medications based on self-diagnosis drawn from Internet research or a TV-commercial-fueled desire for a certain brand of medication, we often see a person given an antidepressant when they're really suffering from an anxiety disorder (and vice versa). Medication is too often perceived as a quick fix, to the exclusion of other possible—and necessary—care.

One-dimensional treatment answers. There's an old saying: "If all you have is a hammer, everything looks like a nail." In the context of medical care, that means physicians who are trained to think that all disease is the result of a biochemical malfunction in the body will naturally reach for one-time "magic pill" fixes, excluding other options. I should say at the outset that I have high regard for skilled, compassionate physicians. But my work with hundreds of depressed clients has caused me great concern about the typical medical model of treatment. Often medical practitioners ignore alternative causes for chronic depression and quickly prescribe a pill as the cure-all. Despite current research showing that many other wellness factors affect our mood—such as gut health, sleep patterns, inflammation in the body, and behavioral habits—a disappointing majority of professionals continue to limit analysis and treatment to what's going on in a patient's gray matter.

Shortsighted self-help books. The problem is made worse by self-help books that overwhelmingly reinforce this narrow approach. That is, they see depression as purely a problem in the brain that can be resolved through cognitive or mood therapy and/or with drugs designed to affect the brain's chemical makeup. Such books have sold well thanks to the many thousands, even millions, of readers who have successfully used these methods to heal. However, their effectiveness is mostly limited to people with mild depression or the regular "blues." Those conditions certainly form part of the depression epidemic, and techniques that address them make a valuable contribution. But they also leave millions of Americans who suffer from more serious and chronic forms of depression out in the cold.

Toxic emotions. Before reaching for typical medical treatments, it's important to examine what I call the "three deadly emotions"—anger, fear, and guilt. Chances are if someone is struggling with depression, he or she is also suffering from the unhealthy influence of one or more of these emotions.

Unresolved hurt, for example, often manifests itself as anger in relationships and can diminish a person's capacity for intimacy, which leads to isolation, bitterness, and resentment. Anger directed inward is a common fuel for self-destructive behaviors like addictions and eating disorders.

Fear typically begins as ordinary worry, the normal "what ifs?" we all experience. But those can spiral out of control, turning into anxiety, panic attacks, and eventually generalized anxiety disorder—a common breeding ground for depression.

Guilt comes in two forms: true guilt, when a healthy and emotionally developed person knows he or she has done something wrong; and false guilt, which is unwarranted and leads to shame. From there, it's a short step to feeling broken, unworthy of love, or otherwise "defective"—all precursors to depression.

Unforgiveness. One of the most universal contributing factors to depression in our clients—which is often not explored by other treatment providers—is entrenched resentment or an inability to forgive. The negative emotions that linger when a person hasn't forgiven someone can create a state of chronic depression, which damages the body on multiple levels. We have seen such strong evidence that these factors play key roles in depression that our treatment approach routinely includes shining a light on those dark, secret places.

Distractions and addictions. While technology has enabled us to create more community ties and stay in touch with far-flung loved ones, the disturbing and largely unexplored reality is that technology also promotes distinct patterns of isolation and social conflict that contribute to depression. Many of our guests at The Center exhibit all the signs of withdrawal from a physical addiction after just a few days without their electronic devices.

Other addictions play a role in depression as well—some of which are hidden from view, like dependency on prescription painkillers or illicit drugs. Still others fall into the category of "soft addictions," such as overeating, shopping, gambling, television viewing, video game playing, oversleeping, and online connectivity. Depression frequently goes hand in hand with addictions of some kind. Facing them, and starting the recovery process in those areas, is critical to success in healing from depression.

Physical pollutants in the body. Few people are aware that common chemicals in our diet, like artificial sweeteners and preservatives, are actually neurotoxins that build up in the body and interfere with our health. In treating depression, it's vital to find and eliminate these hidden sources of stress.

Whole-Person Healing

As you can see, depression is not limited to what's happening in your head. Far from it! Numerous factors have contributed to the onset and severity of your depression, and each of these must be addressed throughout the healing process as well. That's what I call the whole-person model of treatment. To illustrate the idea, here's a story that's typical of many clients we see at The Center.

John came to us in his early forties with severe depression. He'd been depressed for a long time, but his symptoms had grown significantly worse in recent years. By the time he checked into The Center, he rarely left his house, was a hundred pounds overweight, had major digestive upset, and was taking multiple medications—three for depression, one for anxiety, and a variety of over-the-counter meds to help settle his gut. Looking for help, he'd "done it all," he told us, like so many of our guests.

But years of traditional therapy and visits to various medical specialties had led to disjointed and ineffective care. Based on a careful review of his files, it was clear he had gotten some good advice here and there, but in treating his diverse medical problems, the assortment of practitioners he'd seen had never asked this one simple question: "What's going into your mouth every day?"

Yes, he talked to more than a few doctors about his rapid weight gain and the effect it had on other physical problems, but those conversations usually had gone something like this:

"You know you need to lose some weight."

"Yeah, I know I need to lose some weight."

"You need to eat better."

"Yeah, I know I need to eat better."

Round and round it went. But circling an issue means you never get to the core of the problem, something the whole-person approach aims to avoid.

What we found during John's intake assessment shocked us. He was self-employed and worked from home, a fact that allowed him to hide an incredible addiction: John consumed an average of twelve pots of coffee a day. Not twelve *cups*. Twelve *pots*. He shared with me that no one had ever asked him how much coffee he drank, so he had never thought to mention it before.

So, in addition to his depression, John had evolved numerous other issues that were directly undermining his recovery. All that caffeine had rinsed the B vitamins out of his system, severely upset the balance of "good" bacteria in his gut, and derailed his appetite, causing him to binge eat large amounts of sugar. That, in turn, caused hypoglycemia. Since coffee had become his only fluid intake, his body settled into a state of permanent dehydration, degrading his mental acuity and other bodily functions at the cellular level. And yet, despite how horrible he felt, he was seriously dependent on coffee.

"I need it just to help me get through the day," he insisted.

Over the next few weeks, we helped John to rehydrate his body.

("One bottle of water for every cup of coffee.") Eventually, his coffee intake dropped to three cups a day—and none after 10:00 a.m. Once a week he got an IV bag full of vitamins, minerals, and amino acids, which activated his brain chemistry. His cravings started to decrease, especially for sugar and caffeine. For the first time in years, John began eating a healthy breakfast and lunch. He steadily lost weight, and his energy levels and sense of well-being increased measurably each week.

We practice "mindful walking" at The Center. When John arrived, he could not make it even halfway around the block, saying things like "It takes energy just to breathe." At the end of a month, he was walking six laps every day. The physical changes improved his self-esteem and sense of hope. He walked out of our clinic speaking with optimism, gratitude for being alive, and confidence in a better future.

The last time I spoke with John, he reported doing remarkably better than just a year prior. He'd lost even more weight and sustained his increased physical activity through tennis, a sport he loved but had abandoned years ago when it became too difficult to leave his house. His business improved along with his mood, and he was down to one medication for depression.

This is what whole-person treatment looks like in practice: working together on multiple healing fronts all at once. Often our patients have never suspected a connection between their depression and other factors like sleep quality, technology use, nutrition, lifestyle, and behavioral health issues. It comes as a surprise when we ask them to think outside the traditional treatment box and address the whole mental health matrix, not just a single factor.

The "Why Not?" Approach

My response to reluctant strugglers is to ask, "What have you got to lose?" And I'm asking you the same thing now. In the following pages,

I'll suggest things you might never have tried before in your attempts to be free of depression. Some will challenge you in unexpected ways. Some will test your resolve by asking you to address old wounds, thought patterns, and addictions. I'll be honest with you: none of these remedies fall into the category of "magic bullet" or "quick fix." They'll require you to buy in and commit—just as I did years ago when I realized I needed to set boundaries for my recovery. No one could do that part but me. It takes courage, perseverance, and an open mind. My approach is not to throw multiple things against the wall and see what sticks. The whole-person plan is a proven method that works. For thirty years, I've watched people desperate for help and without hope find themselves again, regaining the vitality and buoyancy that had been submerged due to months or years of depression.

Healing depression is not only possible; it is achievable. But it will require taking a hard look at your life and adjusting your lifestyle—in some cases, permanently. The whole-person plan is not a magic bullet, nor is it a once-for-all fix. The road to wellness is less like a detour back to where you were going and more like following a new road to a new destination.

I expect healing to be hard work, but it's worth it. Begin this journey by asking yourself, *Why not?*

- If healing from depression is a thousand-piece puzzle, why not find all the pieces and put them in place so the picture of your life is whole again?
- If you've tried everything else you can think of to be well, why not try the things you haven't yet thought of?
- If you're truly sick and tired of being sick and tired, why not go all in with a full-spectrum housecleaning of your life?
- If you feel ready to abandon hope, why not ask for help—from family, friends, and professionals who can also learn from a whole-person point of view?

- Most of all, why not seek God's help? Spiritual factors are often overlooked in traditional treatment for depression, but no one knows better how to restore you to health than God.

You were not born to suffer or to barely survive. You were born to thrive. The time will never be more right to begin your journey back to abundant wellness.

As you look forward, the path may seem impassable, an impossible climb over the pain, despair, and depletion you've been burdened with for so long. I encourage you to imagine instead standing on the crest of that mountain, vibrant and victorious, looking to the bright horizon ahead. Can you picture that? I know you can! Let's get going together.

CHAPTER 1

Finding a New Path Forward

Why Lasting Healing Can Feel like an Unreachable Mirage

We've all heard it before: "Depression is all in your head! Just give it time." Or worse, "Snap out of it already!"

This kind of advice is rarely loving or helpful—though, like the broken clock that is accurate twice a day, it occasionally manages to be sort of right. That is, for people who are experiencing an ordinary case of the blues or temporary emotional upheaval due to grief or trauma, time can be an ally, and natural mental resiliency usually does return in due course.

But for millions of people around the world, those more common scenarios are unfamiliar. These individuals are caught in the grip of something larger and more tenacious than that. They suffer from clinical depression, and no amount of glib advice is going to make it "go away." So, here at the beginning of our journey into *Healing Depression for Life*, let's orient ourselves on the map and all agree on a common starting point:

Depression is real. And painful. And frightening.

All too often, depression can even be life threatening when it drains a person of hope to the point of considering self-harm. Beyond the toll it takes on individual lives, depression places enormous strain on families, businesses, schools, and governments. In fact, no corner of society is immune to its disabling effects. That's true across the globe, not just in America. According to a World Health Organization (WHO) bulletin, "More than 300 million people are now living with depression, an increase of more than 18% between 2005 and 2015."[1] WHO further estimates that "substance abuse and mental disorders," including depression, are the world's number one cause of disability—the loss of normal function at home and work.

Here at home, the 2016 National Survey on Drug Use and Health revealed that 16.2 million adults and 3.1 million adolescents between ages 12 and 17 had endured a recent "major depressive episode." Around two-thirds of those people suffered life impairments that were rated as "severe." However, approximately 37 percent of these adults and a staggering 60 percent of young people received no treatment of any kind, according to the survey.[2]

To make matters worse, research in recent years has revealed that, of those who do seek help, approximately one-third receive little or no lasting benefit from treatments commonly used today.[3] Think about that for a moment: one in three people sees little or no long-term benefit from common treatments for depression. Clearly, the typical approaches offer very limited lasting benefits.

According to the National Institute for Mental Health, symptoms of depression include the following:

- persistent sad, anxious, or "empty" mood
- feelings of hopelessness or pessimism
- feelings of guilt, worthlessness, or helplessness

- loss of interest or pleasure in hobbies or activities
- decreased energy, fatigue, or being "slowed down"
- difficulty concentrating, remembering, or making decisions
- difficulty sleeping, early-morning awakening, or oversleeping
- appetite and/or weight changes
- thoughts of death or suicide or suicide attempts
- restlessness or irritability
- persistent physical symptoms such as aches or indigestion[4]

At The Center: A Place of Hope, we believe that if a person reports a chronic combination of these symptoms lasting sixty to ninety days—far beyond what's expected in cases of the ordinary blues we all experience from time to time—then he or she is in need of coordinated care for major depression.* Our admissions specialists assess the severity of depression in those seeking help using three criteria: hopelessness, helplessness, and despair. Once a person's experience can be characterized by words as bleak as these, they have long lost the ability to "snap out of it."

That so many people do reach this point in their lives makes depression a human tragedy of stunning proportions.

No More Quick Fixes

Now that we've established the magnitude of the problem, let's agree on a vastly more important fact: *it doesn't have to be this way.* Healing is possible, now and for good. So why do we continue to fall so short? Why do even the lucky ones with access to care so often come away disappointed?

While the answers to these questions are far from simple, they don't take an advanced degree in medicine to understand. There is a certain lack of common sense at the root of the problem. Once you've

---

* You can find a self-assessment for depression symptoms in appendix 1 on page 205.

seen that fact, there in plain sight, the mud starts to settle and the view becomes clearer.

Here's one way to get your head around it. Imagine you take your car to the shop. It's hard to describe to the mechanic exactly what seems to be going wrong. The best you can do is to say, "It's just not right." The engine doesn't fire right up in the morning the way it used to. There's no pep anymore when you hit the accelerator. The steering is sluggish and unresponsive, and the tires inexplicably lose air no matter how often you refill them. The heater is stuck at lukewarm, and all the radio speakers sound muffled, ruining your favorite music. You used to love this car. Now it's no fun to drive at all.

As you conclude your list of the car's "symptoms," the mechanic nods sagely and assures you he knows just what's causing the trouble. "You need a tune-up!" he says, with great confidence. You are not the expert, so you take his word for it. "Come back tomorrow, and everything will be back to normal."

You can see where this story is headed. The next day after the repair work, you start the engine to head home and discover that nothing has changed. In fact, you feel worse about things, because now you're out the cost of a tune-up and the time spent waiting for the work to be done. You turn around and tell the mechanic to try again. And so, day after day, the list of ineffective repairs grows longer and longer, and you feel further and further away from your goal. Discouragement sets in, and you're about to give up on the prospect of ever driving a functional car again.

The problem is easy to see in this made-up example: *the mechanic is assuming the car's troubles are caused by just one thing.* Instead of looking at the vehicle's systems as an integrated, interdependent whole, he has been trained to see it only as a collection of separate parts. Repair, in his view, is about fixing the broken piece, period. No need to look in the trunk for problems he's sure are under the hood.

Not only that, *the mechanic sees your car only in light of all the others he's worked on lately.* Last week, a Chevrolet came in with some of the same troubles and, lo and behold, the tune-up worked! Suddenly, to him, all cars that have lost their pep fall into the same category and require the same treatment.

Now, please don't think I'm disrespecting mechanics or the caregivers they represent in this little fable. Nearly everything they are trained to do is effective under the right circumstances. Sometimes a tune-up is exactly what's called for. But if it becomes a one-size-fits-all solution to every malfunction—no matter how complex or multifaceted its causes and no matter the differences between individual automobiles—that's an approach sure to lead to as many failures as successes. Maybe even more.

Treatment Is a Team Effort

That's what has become of standard treatments for depression these days. Care providers tend to use their favorites as singular fixes for a disorder that is never caused by one thing alone. In my experience, depression always arises from multiple factors converging in a person's life. Treating one thing at a time, with one method at a time, is akin to expecting new tires to revitalize a car with multiple systems on the blink.

Below is a list of commonly prescribed depression treatments these days—and the reasons why each on its own is unlikely to produce lasting healing.

Medication

More than thirty years ago, on December 29, 1987, the US Food and Drug Administration approved the antidepressant drug fluoxetine, now well known by its trade name, Prozac. The first drug of its kind, it marked a radical shift in how depression is treated in the world. Prozac belongs to a class of drugs called selective serotonin reuptake inhibitors (SSRIs) that is thought to increase levels of the neurotransmitter serotonin by interfering with the body's ability to reabsorb it from the bloodstream. Scientists theorize that a lack of serotonin is at least partly responsible for symptoms of depression.

The discovery of SSRI drugs—and now there are many different versions on the market—was hailed as a revolution in the treatment of depression and other mental disorders. But in the intervening years, while antidepressant medications continue to be widely pre-scribed and many people do derive some benefit from their use, evidence has mounted that they are not the "magic bullet" doctors once hoped they would be. Here are a handful of reasons why:

- In numerous studies, SSRIs performed only marginally better than placebos.
- Patients taking antidepressants show roughly the same improvement as those being treated with talk therapy alone.
- Between 65 and 80 percent of people on antidepressants relapse into depression within a year.
- SSRIs carry side effects for many people, some of which are significant. These include trouble sleeping, sexual dysfunction, loss of appetite, dry mouth, rash, abnormal dreams, and more serious effects like seizures and an increased risk of suicide.
- It is now recognized that discontinuing the use of SSRIs can be difficult, similar to withdrawal from other addictive drugs.

Don't misunderstand: I am not opposed to the use of medications, which can sometimes stabilize an individual enduring an acute crisis. Further, I am privileged to work in conjunction with many brilliant, caring physicians who skillfully use pharmaceuticals as part of their therapeutic regimen. I believe antidepressant medications have a vital role to play in recovery for many people. They can calm the chaos of a major depressive episode to give you a chance to rest and regain your footing. What they can't do is fix the reasons you became depressed in the first place—and that is perhaps the biggest drawback of all.

Underlying the use of antidepressant medications is a mostly unspoken but powerful medical philosophy that asserts the problem is largely (if not entirely) biochemical in nature. For many decades, the medical establishment has regarded psychology and psychiatry with suspicion, calling these fields "soft science." That's because measuring mental health or dysfunction is not as simple as tracking physical markers and manifestations. Doctors trained in strict biological models are more comfortable with mechanical causes and cures for illness—even mental disorders. Some distrust talk therapy or behavior adjustment as inherently untestable. ("It's all in your head" takes on a different meaning in this context.)

Once a person accepts this view and starts taking medication with the expectation that "everything will be fine now," then doctors and patients alike stop considering all the other causes and remedies we now know have a role to play. These are the puzzle pieces we look for in the whole-person model of treatment: diet, other medications, built-up toxins in the body, physical conditions, life circumstances, emotional environment (past and present), allergies, spirituality, sleep habits, addictions, and more. Uncovering and correcting problems in these areas of your life takes commitment, sacrifice, and work, so it's easy to see the appeal of a pill that does it all for you.

Talk Therapy

Again, it's important to understand that there are many gifted therapists in the world doing excellent work to provide hope and healing to their clients. I have great admiration for caring, trained therapists who consistently offer wisdom and compassion to their clients. These professionals create a healing space where a person can feel safe—perhaps for the first time—to explore painful wounds from the past or confront present-day circumstances that are intolerable. Like the car tune-up, this may be exactly what someone needs who is suffering a typical case of doldrums or who is in the process of recovering from the grief of loss.

But for those in the grip of major depression—remember, these are people who are hopeless, helpless, and despairing—talk therapy alone is unlikely to produce lasting relief and healing. Here's why:

- Talk therapy rarely integrates a thorough exploration of physical conditions that contribute to depression.
- Talk therapy is generally a slow process, which is not always suitable for someone who may be considering suicide or who is sliding toward an inability to function on a basic level.
- Talk therapy tends to look backward, searching for old wounds to account for current patterns of thought and behavior. Most often we find plenty of immediate causes in our patients, things that can be addressed here and now.

Working through deep issues with a therapist can be an outstanding component of a whole-person treatment plan, one of many simultaneous avenues for healing. As powerful and helpful as counseling can be, I still believe it should be utilized among other treatment approaches to experience lasting progress in overcoming depression.

Cognitive Behavioral Therapy (CBT)

While psychotherapy is focused on understanding the root causes of a person's symptoms—often buried out of sight in the subconscious mind—CBT is chiefly concerned with developing strategies for managing those symptoms right now. The idea is to help people see that changing distorted thoughts, beliefs, and attitudes about themselves, others, and the future can have a direct effect on how they feel about those things. Distorted thinking is usually accompanied by maladaptive behaviors that can likewise be reprogrammed to improve a person's outlook.

Research has shown that CBT alone is at least as effective as antidepressant medication at treating less severe forms of depression, but it is usually recommended in combination with drugs for people experiencing more severe symptoms. Once more, it's clear that CBT has an important role to play, but used in isolation it has the following shortcomings:

- CBT ignores underlying medical conditions that contribute to depression.
- CBT does not address environmental factors, such as exposure to toxins and electromagnetic radiation.
- Being focused on reducing present-day symptoms, CBT does not consider depressive emotions like fear, anger, and guilt or the toxic effect of refusing to forgive someone for a perceived offense.
- As a treatment for depression, CBT is less likely to find and deal with associated mental conditions, such as addiction or anxiety.

Pray (or Meditate) It Away

Seeking spiritual connection is a powerful and effective part of any healing strategy for people with depression—or anyone else, for that matter. It is absolutely a part of the whole-person model. God truly is the Great Physician.

I want you to know that I believe wholeheartedly in prayer, and in fact, I pray to the God I have faith in nearly every day. What's more, I have witnessed countless answers to prayers in my own life and in the lives of others. As you'll see in part 2, spiritual practices are a central part of the whole-person approach I advocate.

My concern arises when people suffering from depression rely *only* on prayer, at the exclusion of other resources available to assist in their healing. Prayer without appropriate attention to other obvious avenues for wellness runs the same risks as other single-focus approaches. If you believe prayer by itself is all you need to heal, you may be less likely to explore your diet, sleep habits, possible addictions, toxic chemicals lurking in your home, harmful emotions that hold you captive, and so on. Spiritual resources are meant to empower you in confronting and changing all those kinds of things, not to distract you from the need to deal with them. I encourage my clients (and myself) to pray especially for wisdom and guidance in dealing with life's many challenges, including depression.

But the most important reason why prayer as a solitary healing strategy can disappoint you in the end is that it runs the risk of deepening your sense of unworthiness and failure—emotions that are key contributors to depression. The inner dialogue goes something like this: *If I were a better Christian (or a more spiritual person), I wouldn't be depressed in the first place. So to turn this thing around, I will double down and be the best child of God I can possibly be.*

Or maybe this: *God, I know I have failed miserably to be joyful and thankful for your many blessings. Please forgive me and help me to heal.*

If these prayers are not accompanied by a commitment to do the work of improving lifestyle choices—for example, examining eating habits and possible addictions and letting go of old fears and wounds—then healing is likely to be inhibited, just as with other singular approaches. Then what happens? Your sense of guilt and even shame stands to deepen, making matters worse.

Nothing at All

Earlier in this chapter, you read the troubling fact that 37 percent of adults and 60 percent of adolescents suffering from depression receive no treatment of any kind. In many cases that's because access to care is limited for geographic or financial reasons. But just as often, people don't get the care they need because they don't seek it out, or refuse it when offered. The perceived social stigma of needing help with a mental health issue is still a powerful deterrent for many people. Others have suffered for so long that they are convinced healing depression is impossible, so why bother trying? For these people, living with depression has become the new normal, with the assumption that they'll always feel miserable, so it's best to accept it and muddle on.

Clearly, there's no need to list the obvious limitations of this way of dealing with depression. If this has been your approach in the past, please keep reading! I hope to convince you that healing is not only possible but it's also probable if you're willing to look deeply at all the puzzle pieces that may be currently out of place in your life. Ask yourself, what stigma can there be in gaining control of your diet or your sleep habits, in confronting your fear, anger, and guilt? Why not examine how a lack of forgiveness is making you ill? What have you got to lose?

A Way out of the Dark

When searching for effective ways to treat and heal from depression, we should be looking not for the one smoking gun but rather for all the missing puzzle pieces. My purpose in discussing the limitations of various treatments when they are employed one at a time is not to criticize highly trained caregivers who are passionate about helping people heal or to suggest anyone should discontinue a treatment pathway that is working. But it also benefits no one for us to ignore the mounting evidence that genuine, lasting healing from depression can be achieved only through integrated, multifaceted approaches that give attention to the whole person.

In the coming chapters, we will look at the whole person to discover what factors might be contributing to your depression and how you can holistically address those factors. The book is divided into "Mind," "Soul," and "Body," as each of these areas plays a crucial role in your being able to understand and heal from depression. While it may be tempting to jump around, and while the chapters can be read independently, I would encourage you to consider each chapter. As already discussed, treatment is a team effort, and just as it is helpful when looking at individual puzzle pieces to see the picture on the box, you will likely have a better understanding of yourself and your needs if you are armed with all the information in this book.

If you are suffering from depression, or someone you love is, chances are you've come to this book because you've tried other options that left you disappointed and discouraged. The purpose of this chapter is to say, "Take heart!" If previous treatments have not worked for you, the fault does not lie with you but with the common—and mistaken—belief that any *one* drug or process can hold all the answers. Take heart, because the rest of this book will show you how to succeed where other attempts have let you down.

Your Personal Action Plan

By now it should be obvious that the whole-person model will challenge you to give up false hope in "magic bullets." The treatment ideas in the pages ahead will ask you to work hard, dig deep, and above all, become an active participant in your journey to wellness.

Here are five ways to get started today:

1. **Begin the process of self-assessment by taking inventory of your life.** Look for habits, lifestyle choices, circumstances, emotions, attitudes, and medical conditions that will need more attention as you move deeper into whole-person treatment. Make a word picture of your life. Be honest and courageous. Write down everything that comes to mind.

2. **Educate yourself.** Don't just take my word for it. There are ample sources of good information about the merits and pitfalls of common treatments for depression and the value of an integrated approach to healing. Some of those helpful sources are presented at the end of this book (see appendix 4). Make use of them!

3. **Talk to your current caregivers.** Inquire about the relative strengths and weaknesses of various treatment types. Let them know you are interested in broadening your approach to healing.

4. **Pay attention to your thoughts and beliefs.** Carefully assess what can work and what can't. Do you secretly scoff at the idea that diet affects mental health? Are you already convinced that other possible addictions—like imbalanced use of technology or shopping or pornography—have no role to play in depression? If so, you're unlikely to give those things the attention they need in the pursuit of lasting healing. Make a list of such limiting thoughts. About each one, ask yourself: *Why do I think this way? Is this the truth? How is it holding me back?*

5. **Write out a history of things you've tried already to help you heal from depression.** Chances are you'll see how each attempt to feel better stands apart from others, rarely working together. You'll also notice all the things you haven't yet tried . . . which is great news! It means you're not out of options after all.

PART 1

Mind

CHAPTER 2

Sound Asleep

The Curative Power of a Solid Night's Sleep

Jennifer used to love her life. She had a challenging career as a software developer, a husband and three children she adored, and a supportive network of family and friends. Her family lived in a nice home in a Dallas suburb with frequent block parties and barbecues. Jennifer's life seemed picture perfect, and for a long time she would have agreed with that description.

Then everything changed.

Looking back, she could pinpoint when the shift occurred. She remembered a five-month period during which grief was her constant companion. Losing a childhood friend to breast cancer and a colleague to suicide five weeks later left Jennifer reeling. A few months later, the death of her ninety-two-year-old grandmother, while not unexpected, was another huge loss. That fall, when Jennifer's seven-year-old son was diagnosed with type 1 diabetes, something in Jennifer felt broken beyond repair.

And so began a two-year spiral that culminated in Jennifer coming to The Center desperate for relief. In my first consultation with Jennifer, I asked her to describe her symptoms. In addition to fatigue, alternative bouts of feeling sad and numb, and being unable to focus at work, she told me she was suffering from insomnia. For several months, her sleep routine had been disrupted as she woke up nearly every night at three o'clock, only to stare at the ceiling and listen to her husband's steady breathing beside her as he slept soundly. Sometimes she would eventually fall back to sleep, sometimes not. In the morning she would get up, bleary eyed and foggy headed, and "trudge through the day like a zombie," as she described it.

Each night, Jennifer would face the same miserable scenario all over again, like a dreadful recurring scene from the movie *Groundhog Day*. Naturally, as her sleep problems persisted week after week, her depression worsened.

Although I felt deeply sympathetic toward Jennifer as she explained her desperate situation, I wasn't at all surprised. Over several decades of working with depressed individuals, I've come to recognize that the vast majority of them suffer from sleep issues that turn into sleep disorders. It seems like a cruel irony: at a time when these people are struggling to regain stability and find a shred of hope, peaceful and restorative sleep eludes them.

The relationship between sleep and depression isn't discussed as often as, say, symptoms of sadness or fatigue. And yet, after working with literally thousands of depressed patients, I know that sleep is virtually always a part of the problem and, more important, must be an integral part of the solution.

An Epidemic of Sleep Problems

Before we examine the profound connection between sleep issues and depression, I want to look at some of the factors that make this such a growing concern. A study by the CDC shows that more than a third of adults and more than two-thirds of teenagers do not get enough sleep.[1] Undoubtedly, you've had your own experiences with sleepless nights, so the intensity of this problem is probably not surprising to you.

What may come as a surprise, however, is the pervasiveness of the problem, as well as one of the driving forces behind it. The decline in sleep quality for Americans has been called nothing short of an epidemic, and one of the dynamics fueling this epidemic is our ever-growing obsession with technology (a topic we will discuss in the next chapter).

A 2011 poll by the National Sleep Foundation revealed some disturbing trends. The study showed that nearly four in ten Americans regularly bring their cell phones into their bedrooms and use them right before trying to fall asleep. The numbers skyrocket to roughly seven in ten when we look specifically at teens and adults under the age of thirty.[2]

Why is this bad news? Let's look at the impact of something as seemingly harmless as texting right before bedtime. According to the same National Sleep Foundation poll, people who text in the hour before trying to fall asleep even a few nights a week are

- less likely to report getting a good night's sleep,
- more likely to wake up feeling unrefreshed,
- more likely to be categorized as "sleepy" on the Epworth Sleepiness Scale, and
- more likely to drive drowsy.[3]

Why are cell phones, computers, televisions, and other devices in the bedroom so detrimental to healthy sleep patterns? There are several reasons:

- Let's start with the obvious: our cell phones wake us up in the middle of the night. The beeps and chimes that keep us connected during the day—calendar alerts, texts, phone calls, e-mail notifications, weather alerts—don't necessarily stop when we turn off the lights.
- Being exposed before bedtime to even small amounts of the light emitted by electronic devices makes it harder to fall asleep and stay asleep. This is because the shortwaves interfere with the body's natural production of melatonin, the hormone that controls our circadian rhythm, or cycles of sleeping and waking.
- Using technology right before sleep is both physiologically and psychologically stimulating. Flinders University professor Michael Gradisar concludes in his research that interactive media—including video games and social media sites—arouse and activate the brain in ways that noninteractive media, such as movies, do not.[4] Gradisar also contributed to a review of thirty-six papers on the relationship between sleep and electronics, which established a consistent link between the use of media at bedtime and delayed onset of sleep as well as shortened sleep time.[5]

Another dynamic that must be considered is the rise in prescription drug use. A study by researchers at the Mayo Clinic revealed that seven out of ten Americans take a prescription drug, and one in five US patients is on five or more prescription drugs—many of which include insomnia among their side effects.[6]

The fact that some medications disrupt sleep cycles is an important piece in the puzzle. Offending drugs can include medications related to past illnesses as well as concurrent illnesses and even a morass of depression medications that may have unwanted side effects. The list of prescription medications that can interfere with a healthy night's sleep includes heart medications, asthma medications, antidepressants, and nicotine patches, as well as medications for ADHD and hypothyroidism. Over-the-counter pain medications and decongestants have also been linked with insomnia.

Why does this matter? It matters because when we don't get enough sleep, our bodies, brains, and emotions are impacted, and we experience the following:

- decreased overall activity in the brain, affecting learning, memory, attention, and productivity
- impaired driving performance and response times like the impairments experienced while driving intoxicated
- interference with healthy heart function
- compromises in how the body repairs joint and muscle injuries
- reduced production of the hormones the body uses to control appetite, leading to increased obesity
- greater cognitive and behavior issues experienced by people with dementia[7]

As if these outcomes weren't disruptive enough, when we consider what research continues to reveal about the link between inadequate sleep and depression and even suicidal ideations, we can no longer underestimate the healing power of sleep in the life of anyone suffering in a depressive state.

A Downward Spiral

If you've ever struggled—or struggle now—to get a good night's sleep, you know how frustrating and discouraging it can be. And you're not alone. If you ask virtually any depressed person about sleep, you will almost certainly hear about distorted and disturbed sleep patterns:

- Among people diagnosed with depression, three out of four struggle with insomnia, while 15 percent report symptoms of hypersomnia (excessive sleepiness during the day, which can occur on its own or with insomnia).
- Nearly 90 percent of people with severe depression struggle with early-morning insomnia.
- Among people who are not depressed, the presence of insomnia indicates a higher risk for depression later in life.[8]

In the introduction I mentioned my own experience with a major depressive episode. During that time in my life, a good night's sleep was rare. I remember lying awake for hours, ruminating on anxious thoughts or watching the numbers change on my bedside clock. Even when the substances I was abusing knocked me out for a night, I would wake up groggy and have a difficult time functioning during the day. Many years later, I felt so passionately about the power of a good night's sleep that I helped design a premium mattress, called The Serenity, along with a sleep-inducing supplement, At Ease PM.

Why are sleep issues so prevalent among people suffering from depression? Sleep studies done with depressed patients have shown that depression changes our sleep architecture. People who are depressed experience an altered sleep cycle, entering REM sleep more quickly and spending less time in sleep stages three and four.[9]

Sleep stages three and four—the stages associated with delta, or slow-wave, brain activity—are often called "priority sleep" because they are so critical to our emotional and physical well-being. Sleep expert Mary O'Brien, MD, explains the power of these two stages in this way:

Many of our body's repair processes occur during slow-wave sleep. Muscles, bones, and joints heal assorted injuries and micro-traumas. Skin and other connective tissues regenerate or repair themselves largely during Stage 3 sleep. During Stage 4 sleep, the anterior lobe of the pituitary gland synthesizes between 70 percent and 80 percent of our total daily allotment of growth hormone [which] helps us maintain normal muscle mass, strength, endurance, and stamina. Without adequate levels of growth hormone, you feel like a dishrag!

Many neurotransmitters are synthesized in Stage 4 sleep, including acetylcholine, critical for memory and learning, dopamine, vital for staying focused and alert, and serotonin and norepinephrine, essential for well-being. No wonder sleep deprivation feels so miserable. When we spend inadequate amounts of time in deep, slow-wave sleep, we deprive our brain of what it needs to produce normal levels of hormones and neurotransmitters.[10]

The link between sleep patterns and depression is so prevalent that at The Center our team performs a sleep study with most of our incoming patients to help determine just how much their sleep quality has deteriorated. But the data is a tricky business. That's because it can be difficult to determine whether a person's sleep issues are symptoms of their depression or whether trouble sleeping has contributed to the rise of depression. It's a chicken-and-egg kind of dilemma: Does a person's depression cause sleep disruption, or does lack of sleep cause depression?

The answer is yes, both. What's more, I have concluded that it doesn't matter which came first, sleep disturbances or depression. Each fuels the other, creating a vicious downward spiral. The critical issue is to improve sleep quality so that depression levels will improve as well.

Addressing Sleep Deprivation

Depression and sleep deficits are unarguably entwined. Yet in that interwoven relationship lie opportunities for treatment, relief, and healing. Indeed, when you take measures to improve the quality of a depressed person's sleep, you also relieve symptoms of his or her depression.

The wisdom in cotreating sleep issues and depression is backed up by study after study. For example, research conducted at the sleep clinic at the Sir Charles Gairdner Hospital in Australia concluded that among their subjects the severity of depressive symptoms was directly correlated with the severity of sleep apnea. The study also observed that when sleep apnea was relieved via CPAP therapy, depressive symptoms were relieved.[11]

Another study involved 545 patients in a randomized controlled trial. One group was given Prozac (for depression) and Lunesta (for sleep), while the control group was given Prozac and a placebo. Compared to the control group, patients who received the Prozac and Lunesta not only saw greater sleep improvements but also showed greater improvements in depressive symptoms than the group that received Prozac alone.[12]

The above studies documented improvements in depression when sleep problems were treated via CPAP therapy and medication. Of even greater interest, I believe, are the cotreatment studies that address the sleep portion of the equation using behavioral changes.

Two studies come to mind. The first, conducted by Dr. Rachel Manber at the Stanford University Medical Center, discovered that after treating sleep issues with cognitive-behavioral therapy (which focuses on changing how a person thinks and responds to situations), the success rate for depression treatment nearly doubled.[13]

A different study showed similar results: after resolving sleep issues with talk therapy, 87 percent of those treated "saw their depression symptoms dissolve," nearly double the rate compared to patients who still suffered from insomnia.[14]

A Natural Approach

At The Center, we gravitate toward the use of natural, nondrug methods to address sleep issues in our depressed clients. While our doctors are not strictly opposed to the use of medications to promote sleep, there is always the possibility that some patients will become psychologically dependent on over-the-counter sleep aids (like Sominex or Tylenol PM). There is also an addictive quality to prescription sleep meds such as Lunesta and Ambien.

This is why I prefer recommending simple, natural methods that have proven to be effective at improving sleep. These methods make up something called *sleep hygiene*, which is the term used to describe behaviors we can adopt that help to promote good sleep.

I am going to give you a list of eleven behaviors you can adopt that will improve the quality of your sleep. You'll notice that the actions on this list don't take place only at night. This is because a good night's sleep doesn't begin an hour or two before bed but is determined by many choices, habits, and behaviors throughout the day. There are many things you can do during your waking hours that will greatly improve the quality of your sleep.

During the Day

1. **Get exposure to natural light.** Exposure to sunlight helps maintain a healthy sleep cycle. In fact, receiving intervals of light and darkness is the method by which our bodies determine our circadian rhythm, or internal clock. Exposure to natural light during the day is especially important for people who may not venture outside much.

2. **Exercise.** Just ten minutes of daily aerobic activity can significantly improve your sleep. Because rigorous exercise circulates endorphins into the body, which can make it harder to fall asleep, I recommend getting your exercise in before midafternoon every day. (We'll discuss this topic at length in chapter 9.)

3. **Take short naps.** While some experts advise against napping because of potential disruption of nighttime sleep patterns, I encourage my clients to catch up on their slumber any time they can. Napping may not make up for a poor night's sleep, but a short nap can still be beneficial. I recommend limiting daytime naps to a half hour, however, so sleeping at night is not compromised.

4. **Review the medications you are taking.** If you suspect that sleep issues are related to a medication you are taking, talk to your physician or pharmacist. Switching medications, changing a dosage, or taking your medication at a different time of day may be options.

As Evening Approaches

1. **Watch what you eat close to bedtime.** It's no secret that heavy, rich, or spicy foods can keep you awake at night. Even citrus fruits and carbonated drinks can trigger indigestion, and too much alcohol close to bedtime can disrupt sleep as the body processes the alcohol. In other words, when it comes to eating and drinking before bed, go easy on anything you consume.

2. **Avoid stimulants close to bedtime.** Coffee is an obvious stimulant, but many people forget that soda and tea can contain caffeine as well. Nicotine and exercise are other stimulants that can keep us from falling quickly into sleep.

I also put emotionally upsetting conversations and activities in this category of things to avoid, as well as exposure to electronics. As discussed earlier in this chapter, even something as innocuous as texting right before bed provides light and stimulation that will undermine the quality of your sleep.

3. **Follow a regular, relaxing bedtime routine.** Maintaining a consistent nightly routine helps the body recognize when it's time to sleep. Your process might include taking a warm shower or bath, reading a book, or listening to soothing music. Your routine should also include going to bed and waking up around the same time. Ideally, you should go to bed and wake up within the same thirty-minute window every day.

    Something else to consider adding to your bedtime routine is the simple act of making a to-do list. Psychologists at Baylor University wanted to find out if writing down future-oriented thoughts would help people sleep better. After recruiting fifty-seven adults for the study, the researchers asked half the group to spend five minutes before bed writing down things they had accomplished in the past few days. The other half of the group was asked to spend five minutes before bed writing down things they needed to remember to do in the coming few days.

    People who wrote the to-do lists fell asleep, on average, nine minutes faster than people who wrote about things they had already accomplished. Baylor University assistant professor of psychology and neuroscience Michael Scullin says, "We think that when people offload everything in their mind that might be hard to remember otherwise, it gives them some relief from that rumination."[15]

4. **Create a comfortable environment.** As evening approaches, make sure you have arranged a peaceful, calming environment for sleeping. Things that help create this atmosphere may

include buying a comfortable mattress and keeping your bedroom cool (between sixty and sixty-eight degrees). It can also include things like earplugs, white noise machines, humidifiers, and fans. And if you have pets that wake you up at night, by all means, keep them out of the bedroom.

5. **Don't watch TV, study, or read in bed.** When you engage in these activities, your brain associates your bed with wakefulness. Just as regular, relaxing bedtime routines can help your brain and body know when it's time for sleep, your bed itself is another important trigger. By helping your brain associate your bed with sleep, the transition into slumber will be much smoother.

At Night

1. **Keep your room as dark as possible.** Remember, our bodies use exposure to light and dark to "set" our internal clocks. Even small amounts of light from lamps, cell phones, TV screens, and digital clocks will interfere. If needed, consider purchasing blackout curtains for your bedroom.

2. **Don't stay in bed awake for more than five to ten minutes.** We all experience times when we find ourselves awake in the middle of the night. Perhaps the mind is racing or we are worried about not being able to sleep or we find ourselves wide awake for no discernable reason at all. Given the need to train our brains to associate our beds with sleeping, lying awake in bed for hours is rarely a good idea. Instead, if you can't fall back asleep within five or ten minutes, get out of bed and sit in a chair in the dark until you feel sleepy, and then climb back in bed. And whatever you do, don't pick up your phone

or turn on the TV. The light will confuse your internal clock and stimulate your brain.

As you seek to improve the quality of your sleep, you may find it helpful to photocopy or print the recommendations above and read them regularly. If you accidentally omit some of them or have a bad night, don't be discouraged—just get back on track the next day. By following these recommendations over the long haul, you'll establish habits that will promote great sleep opportunities and emotional wellness.

Your Personal Action Plan

Hopefully, you're encouraged by what you've just read about the impact of sleep on depression. After all, there are so many things you can do to get a better night's sleep. Take steps toward improved sleep quality by doing the following:

1. **For the next two weeks, keep a sleep log.** Record what time you went to bed, what time you got up in the morning, and whether you experienced sleep disruptions during the night (if so, note how many disruptions and for how long). Also, observe how you felt during the day. Pay attention to any correlations between the quality of your sleep and the quality of your moods.

2. **Conduct a light audit of your bedroom.** Note all sources of light. You'll see big offenders (like digital clocks) right away. Now pay attention to more subtle sources like switches on power strips, the status light on your smoke alarm, a nightlight in the bathroom, or a streetlight outside the bedroom window. Reduce or eliminate what you can. If you haven't done so

already, begin leaving your phone in another room, where the glow or vibrations won't disturb you.

3. **Maintain a regular, relaxing nighttime routine.** Begin your wind-down process at least thirty minutes before going to bed. Write down two or three things you can incorporate into a nightly routine that facilitate relaxation. Keep your list where you can see it during the day as a reminder to follow the same routine each evening.

4. **Assess the sleep hygiene suggestions provided in this chapter.** Choose one of the suggestions you don't utilize and incorporate it over the next week. Then move on to another sound-sleep practice.

5. **Stay on track with accountability and encouragement.** Enlist the help of a "better sleep" ally. Discuss the ideas in this chapter and your personal action plan with your spouse, a family member, a roommate, or a friend. Agree to encourage each other to take small steps toward improved sleep habits. Whether or not your sleep ally struggles with depression, pretty much anyone can profit from a better night's sleep, and your friend will benefit from the mutual encouragement as much as you will.

CHAPTER 3

Your Devices, Your Depression

How Overuse of Technology Erodes Mental Health

Albert Einstein once said, "I fear the day that technology will surpass our human interaction. The world will have a generation of idiots." Or at least that's what you'll read from time to time in memes passed around on the Internet. The problem is, there's no evidence that the legendary visionary and genius ever said any such thing.

This quote—or rather, misquote—is very revealing, because it illustrates two facts that deserve our attention as we contemplate the role technology plays in depression.

The first is society's tendency to distrust or even fear technologies when they are new. People will often latch on to every spurious claim of impending doom and take it as fact. This is nothing new. Socrates himself taught that writing—something we'd hardly recognize as a technology anymore—was sure to "create forgetfulness" and leave us with "only the semblance of truth." Millennia later, printed books earned the scorn of philosophers like Gottfried Wilhelm von Leibniz, who feared that "the horrible mass of books that keeps growing might lead to a fall back into barbarism."

Closer to our time, in the early nineteenth century, many people were quite certain the locomotive train was a doomsday machine since they believed the human body was not made to withstand speeds of thirty miles per hour. The list goes on: the telegraph, the telephone, and the television all drew scorn from a fearful public. We are tempted to laugh at that kind of Chicken Little thinking these days. And yet now it's our turn, as the Internet and smartphones have become the latest targets of this phenomenon.

Don't get me wrong. It's a good thing to investigate all possible consequences of introducing radically new ways of doing things, especially the unintended ones. We need to know what we're getting ourselves into. What we don't need is another reason to feel afraid and powerless. The truth is, technologies are rarely either good or evil in themselves; it's how we use them that adds those flavors.

Which brings us to the second fact worthy of our attention: we'd better be wise in our uses, because technology is not always reliable and is not always our friend. Fire can cook your food or burn down your house, depending on how you employ it. Ultimately, that's good news. It suggests that whether your use of technology is harmful or beneficial is mostly up to you. That's empowering—and a good starting place in our discussion of how your use of technology may be prolonging your struggle with depression.

What We Know

To be honest, research into the link between technology use and depression is a mixed bag. In some ways, that's to be expected when studying something that's so new. Widespread social media use, for instance, is still not yet two decades old. The hypothesized effects of too much screen time are also largely subjective and difficult to measure. It's hard to get definitive answers when we're still not entirely sure what the right questions are.

Nevertheless, numerous studies point to adverse mental health effects on young people when they spend too much time engaged in online activity. Those include an increase in suicidal thoughts, depression, and anxiety. A University of Pittsburgh School of Medicine study on the effects of social media use, for instance, concluded that "exposure to highly idealized representations of peers on social media elicits feelings of envy and the distorted belief that others lead happier and/or more successful lives"—which can *cause* depression, the authors wrote.[1]

There is also an unresolved chicken-and-egg dilemma with some research. Studies report a link between Internet use and emotional disorders like ADHD, borderline personality disorders, and anxiety, but they often can't reliably pinpoint which came first. In other words, does Internet usage impact the onset and severity of mental health issues, or does the presence of those disorders make a person more likely to overuse the Internet? These and other questions remain to be answered.

And yet I can confirm from firsthand experience—after working with hundreds of clients over several decades—that the misuse of technology has a direct impact on the severity of depressive symptoms. It's why I have made addressing this behavior a key part of the whole-person approach to healing. When we welcome clients to The Center on their first day, we ask them to relinquish their electronic devices—anything with a screen—for a certain period of time. The reason is simple: to eliminate distractions. We want people to be as present as possible and focused on their recovery process. We store the devices in an office safe for at least seventy-two hours, and in some cases, for the duration of the clients' stay at the clinic.

By the very next day, we notice something remarkable. Most of those people begin to exhibit classic signs of physical withdrawal from an addictive substance. Almost all become irritable and agitated, sometimes developing sweaty palms and an elevated heart rate. Their bodies are responding to the loss of connection via their devices in ways remarkably similar to quitting drugs or alcohol cold turkey. Clearly, something is out of balance in the role technology is playing in their lives.

If we go back to the research looking for a common thread that can help shed light on this experience—and that will suggest ways to alleviate our clients' distress—we find it easily enough. The key lies in the word *misuse* and in how we define it. In other words, we're back where we started, conceding that technology itself is neither harmful nor beneficial. It's our own choices about how we use technology that will determine our experience.

Hidden Costs

It's not important to decide right now which comes first, digital obsession or emotional depression. What matters is this: if you are already struggling with symptoms of depression, overusing technology can make matters much worse. Here's how.

Addiction

First, some good news: drug, alcohol, and tobacco use among adolescents in the United States has steadily fallen since the 1990s. The bad news? Researchers suspect one reason for that is kids are increasingly substituting technology for these substances as their "drug" of choice. One specialist went so far as to describe the smartphone as "digital heroin" for millennials.[2] That appears to be more than mere hyperbole. Findings suggest the brain reacts similarly to positive feedback on social media, for example, as it does to opioid drugs in the bloodstream.

In the United States, surveys suggest Internet addiction rates of up to 8 percent across the population, possibly much higher in some regions. In South Korea—one of the most "connected" nations on earth—authorities estimate that 10 percent of the country's teenagers suffer from full-blown Internet addiction, prompting the government to declare it a serious health issue. Monthlong residential "rehab camps" have sprung up, some treating as many as five thousand kids a year.[3] Worldwide, health officials estimate as many as 420 million people have become addicted to using the Internet.[4] There is no doubt: this is a real and growing problem that cuts across age, race, and gender demographics; socioeconomic classes; and national borders.

What's at the heart of any addiction is impulse control—that is, the struggle to say no when faced with a choice that could have negative consequences. For those who are already battling depression, this is a big problem. A common response to the distress of depression is to reach for anything that makes you "feel better." With the world at your fingertips via the Internet, the range of self-medication options is practically endless. You are one click away from indulging in impulsive shopping, pornography, and gambling or useless "surfing" or bingeing on entertainment or news. Maybe some or all of that delivers a momentary surge of euphoria . . . with the key word being *momentary*. When it wears off, you want more, and so the cycle of addiction begins.

Of course, as with any addiction, over time the lows grow deeper and the highs not as high, which only reinforces feelings of hopelessness, despair, and worthlessness—all the hallmarks of depression. This is why recovery must include an honest look at the scope of your Internet use and treatment for possible addiction to technology alongside everything else.

Isolation

A ubiquitous feature of practically every Internet activity is that it's *solitary*. Sure, you may be messaging or chatting or gaming with others who are also online, but generally, you are physically alone. This isolation can be damaging in many ways, but two in particular have negative consequences for people suffering from depression.

First, interacting with others only through electronic media filters our communication and strips away a huge range of important nonverbal signals. Researchers estimate that anywhere from 65 to 85 percent of all communication takes place through eye contact, facial expression, hand gestures, body position and posture, and so on. While we can choose our words carefully—and even use language to say things that are utterly untrue—it's nearly impossible to manipulate our subconscious signals. In other words, most of us tell the truth with body language. If you want to know what a person really thinks and who they really are, you have to be in personal contact with them. The Internet may provide the appearance of intimacy, but it's an illusion. Real connection by electronic means is impossible. Essentially, online relationships skip normal development and often create a sense of "instant intimacy," which is not true emotional closeness.

This has negative implications for someone who conducts most or all of their relationships online and is also struggling with depression. That person already feels damaged and deficient, probably convinced that's how everyone else sees them as well. Terse text messages and social media comments alone can easily be interpreted in a way that reinforces this belief, whereas face-to-face contact might include an abundance of nonverbal clues to the contrary. Furthermore, isolation hides the nonverbal cues you would otherwise send, letting people who care about you know that you're in distress and need help.

Second, isolation enables us to create what I call "false personas"—virtual identities we present in cyberspace that bear little resemblance to who we actually are. These alter egos allow us to adopt traits we ordinarily shun in face-to-face relationships: verbal aggression and overly explicit sexual communications, for example.

Or they enable us to hide away all evidence of distress and creeping dysfunction in our real lives.

What a person seeking to heal from depression needs most of all is to focus attention on his or her life as it really is, to take stock of unhelpful conditions in the real world, and to accept support from real people.

Virtual Conflict

Social isolation and its tendency to enable behavioral extremes is a two-way street. It's damaging to indulge in those things yourself but also to be exposed to them coming from others. Cyberbullying, while normally thought of as a problem only among teens, can happen to anyone online. According to the Pew Research Center, 41 percent of US adults report they've been the target of online harassment, including 18 percent who say the incidents were "severe," such as sustained stalking or threats of violence.[5] Remove the filters and feedback that govern in-person communication, and you take away the standards of conduct they are meant to regulate as well.

Here's the bottom line: the last thing a person suffering from depression needs is exposure to a stream of merciless judgments and condemnations masquerading as a chat or a comment. An unhealthy self-image is already a trip wire. Far from diffusing the danger, too much time on the Internet is an invitation to make matters worse.

Discomfort with Solitude and Inactivity

A big reason why human beings are drawn to technology is that it stimulates and activates our brains in a way few other things can. The riveting visual imagery, the fast-paced movement of flickering screens, the commotion and constant motion, and the cacophony of noises all get our brain synapses firing at a rapid pace. Overuse of technology often creates a need for more and more stimulation to keep our brains and emotions satisfied. And so we up the ante, seeking additional time with technology and greater intensity from our electronic interactions.

All of this has an often overlooked consequence: a sense of discomfort and restlessness with solitude, stillness, and silence. As a society, we have largely lost appreciation for quietness and introspection. It is in moments of tranquility that we allow our imaginations the freedom to conceive new ideas. It is in moments of contemplation that we listen for spiritual guidance. It is in moments of unhurried reflection that we come to understand who we are as unique individuals.

Technology frequently creates in us a "need for speed," a hunger for nonstop activity and never-ending action. When this occurs, we forfeit the opportunity to grow and to help others grow. I agree with the words of renowned researcher and author Michael Gurian: "As our lives speed up more and more, so do our children's. We forget and thus they forget that there is nothing more important than the present moment. We forget and thus they forget to relax, to find spiritual solitude, to let go of the past, to quiet ambition, to fully enjoy the eating of a strawberry, the scent of a rose, the touch of a hand on a cheek."[6]

Comparison

It's long been recognized that "keeping up with the Joneses" is a big part of what keeps us all running the "rat race." Those may be outdated phrases these days, but the condition of unhealthy envy they describe is alive and well. It's admittedly difficult to avoid noticing the outward appearances of your neighbor's life—job, car, home, overachieving kids, and adventurous vacations—and comparing them to your own, concluding your neighbor must be better off and happier than you. This comparison game is rigged from the start. Media marketers work overtime to be sure you feel your life is lacking so they can sell you what's missing.

Before the Internet, however, those we compared ourselves to were mostly flesh-and-blood people. They lived down the street or worked down the hall. It was at least possible to see them at their worst as well as at their best. And they numbered in the dozens at the very most.

Now we compare ourselves to thousands, if not millions, of virtual neighbors. And we see only what they allow us to see—photos of their pets, happy dinners with friends, the view from an exotic beach, kids getting academic awards, crossing the finish line at the Boston Marathon. Most of this is posted by people who are "friends" in name only. It's a giant understatement to say that all this adds up to a managed and distorted view of who people really are and how they actually live. And that's before we account for perceptions created by advertisers that can be grossly manipulative, misleading, or outright false.

Those suffering from depression are already poised to believe that their lives don't measure up to the lives of others. The Internet provides persuasive "evidence" they're right about that.

Toxic Content

While much of what you see on the Internet presents an overly rosy view of reality, millions of other sites peddle the opposite extreme: nonstop doom and gloom. It's an alarming parade of war, famine, political strife, social injustice, and environmental catastrophe—almost as if news organizations, bloggers, filmmakers, chat group members, and millions of commenters have conspired to turn whole regions of cyberspace into a scene from Dante's *Inferno*, in which the entrance to hell is inscribed "Abandon hope all ye who enter here!" Spend much time there, and you'll be convinced the world teeters on the edge of calamity and collapse every second of every day.

I believe a steady diet of "digital distortion" is harmful to anyone's mental health and magnifies depression symptoms. It rarely leads to healthy or effective political engagement on important issues. In fact, exposure to "doom porn," as it is sometimes humorously called, simply reinforces feelings of powerlessness and despair. That's why, to a person struggling to overcome serious depression, it's positively toxic. Turning off the spigot and cleaning up the digital sludge is an essential step toward recovery.

Time Warp

A hallmark symptom of serious depression is an inability to keep up with daily responsibilities and obligations. You feel drained of the energy and motivation needed to complete even the most commonplace tasks. Lots of factors converge to make this so, including poor nutrition, lack of exercise, unhelpful sleep habits, and chaotic emotions. An often overlooked item that also belongs on the list is time leakage.

A person who is depressed will spend eight hours avoiding fifteen minutes of cleaning the kitchen by filling the time with every possible distraction. The Internet presents an infinite warehouse of options. One click leads to a hundred more possibilities. Social media is a bottomless pit of posts, likes, follows, and comments, and before you know it, whole days have disappeared. In all that time, you're not simply standing still. For reasons we've already discussed, chances are you've gone backward, deeper down the rabbit hole of hopelessness and despair. Reclaiming your time and how you spend it is a vital step in reclaiming your life from depression.

Physical Stagnation

We've already mentioned that, by definition, most technology use is solitary. Now let's consider the fact that it's also *stationary*. Simple observation will confirm this. A person playing video games will remain in virtually the same position for hours. Someone surfing online will sit hunched over a keyboard, sometimes barely looking up for long periods of time.

Health risks associated with such a sedentary lifestyle are well documented: high blood pressure, heart disease, type 2 diabetes, certain types of cancer, obesity, reduced immune system function—and *depression* and *anxiety*. One study titled "The Benefits of Exercise for the Clinically Depressed" noted that "depressed patients are less fit and have diminished physical work capacity on the order of 80% to 90% of age-predicted norms, which in turn may contribute to other physical health problems."[7]

Putting two and two together, it's easy to see how overuse of technology—inevitably stationary and physically stagnant—will stand in the way of lasting healing from depression.

Disconnect Anxiety

The adverse reaction I described earlier among my clients after they've surrendered their devices is a clear sign of something called FOMO—Fear of Missing Out. When you engage with sources of information like social media or news feeds that are updated instantly and constantly, there is no opportunity to look away, even for an instant, without running the risk of getting left behind. Even more captivating is the desire to receive positive feedback to items you've posted yourself. Every new "like" triggers a real-time boost of dopamine, a neurotransmitter that helps regulate the brain's pleasure and reward centers. Maintaining constant connection is like being hooked to an IV delivering a steady drip of mood-altering drugs.

The more connected you are, the more attention you steal from other important things in your life, like performing well at work, driving safely, interacting with friends and family, or completing an important project. Researchers call this state "continuous partial attention," which can also be termed continuous partial *distraction*. Author and consultant Linda Stone calls it "a desire to be a live node on the network." She writes,

Like so many things, in small doses, continuous partial attention can be a very functional behavior. However, in large doses, it contributes to a stressful lifestyle, to operating in crisis management mode, and to a compromised ability to reflect, to make decisions, and to think creatively. In a 24/7, always-on world, continuous partial attention used as our dominant attention mode contributes to a feeling of overwhelm, over-stimulation and to a sense of being unfulfilled. We are so accessible, we're inaccessible. The latest, greatest powerful technologies have contributed to our feeling increasingly powerless.[8]

There's that word again that has such dramatic negative potential for people suffering from depression: *powerless*. Disconnecting is the path back to empowerment and wellness.

Your Personal Action Plan

There is no need to fear technology in itself. We all know it can be an amazing asset and convenience in our lives. But how we use it is of great importance to anyone determined to heal from depression. Finding balance is a checkpoint we can't afford to ignore. Changing your relationship to the Internet is a big step on the road to getting there.

Here are five ways to start:

1. **Keep an online log to track your digital use for one or two weeks.** You can download an app or set your timer to calculate your time spent online. After tracking your daily use for a week or two, you'll have a good idea of how much time you spend connected via the Internet. Brace yourself! Most of us underestimate how much time we spend online, similar to

alcoholics who underestimate or minimize their alcohol consumption. This exercise is not intended to cause you guilt but to provide a reality check about your technology use.

2. **Also track your interaction with other technology.** Because of the prevalence of the Internet in our society, it gets much of the research attention. But of course that's just one source of technology among many. Monitor how many hours you spend watching television, playing video games, viewing movies, and so on. Brace yourself again! Adding these hours to your online hours will probably come as a shock.

3. **Put yourself on a tech diet.** Now that you know your average weekly technology usage, begin to scale back. Start slowly, trimming a half hour from your daily use, then an hour, then more until you achieve a reasonable and comfortable level. The most effective strategy is replacement therapy, meaning you can replace your technology use with enjoyable activities that productively occupy that time: walking with a friend, going to the gym, playing board games with family members, reading a book, tending your garden, or taking up a new hobby (such as tennis, painting, or fly-fishing).

4. **Commit to a periodic digital detox.** This means you will set aside a certain period to interact with absolutely no technology. This might be a full day, a weekend, or a week. For many people, this kind of detox will be difficult; for other people, it sounds downright impossible. But it's not only possible; it is also a positive step toward emotional health. Expect plenty of agitation and restlessness. As said earlier, setting aside your devices often causes a sense of withdrawal, akin to drug withdrawal symptoms. Don't dismiss how difficult a digital detox can be—but also how liberating it can be.

5. **Curtail social media engagement.** Checking Facebook, Instagram, and other sites every other day (or less frequently) should suffice. It's wonderful to keep up with the activities of friends and family members, but let's be honest—most posts and notifications could be skipped without missing anything important. Also, be aware of "friends" who put forth a perfect, polished online presence. You don't need to view posts that cause you to feel envious or inferior.

CHAPTER 4

Stressed and Depressed

*How to Tame Chronic Stress
and Regain Emotional Wellness*

If someone had asked Kelley to describe the last twenty years of her life, two words would have come immediately to her mind:

Survival mode.

Twenty years ago, Kelley was trying to survive an emotionally abusive marriage. When she finally made the decision to leave, she became enmeshed in a grueling and bitter divorce. Then came the financial stress of trying to start a business to support herself and her three children.

Her stress continued to escalate when her ex-husband decided he needed a two-year "break" from paying child support, throwing the family further into financial disarray. Eventually, Kelley hired a family law attorney and took her ex back to court. The judge ruled in her favor, ordering the ex to begin paying child support again and providing reimbursement for the months he didn't pay. Finally caught up on months' worth of overdue bills, Kelley was able to stop foreclosure proceedings on her home with less than a month to spare.

By then, her youngest child was in his midteens and discovering the lure of alcohol. For three frightening years, Kelley lived on high alert as she tried desperately to get her son the help he needed, while navigating the strain of her son's many lies and self-destructive choices.

By the time her youngest came to his senses, committed to sobriety, and was back on the track of becoming a well-adjusted young man, Kelley felt like she was taking her first deep breath in many years.

She was grateful that—finally!—life seemed to have leveled out. Her kids were doing well. She was no longer living paycheck to paycheck. For the first time in a long time, she wasn't waking up in a panic and wondering how she was going to get through the day. Her years of living in survival mode had, at last, come to an end.

Yes, when she looked at her circumstances, she could see that something in her life had shifted dramatically for the better. She couldn't deny she had entered a new chapter of her life. The threats and dangers that had besieged her for years—an abusive husband, financial hardship, a troubled child—had finally subsided.

Still, Kelley soon realized she had little optimism about the future or enthusiasm for her improved lifestyle. Instead of embracing this new season with joy, Kelley felt herself disengaging from everyone around her. As her isolation grew, she battled increasingly negative thoughts, and her emotions continued their steady decline into what felt like an endless abyss of sadness.

The Science of Stress

The idea that long-term stress and depression are linked goes back many decades. Numerous research studies conclusively demonstrate the detrimental effects of prolonged stress on our emotional and physiological well-being. But you don't need to read medical journals to understand the damaging connection between stress and depression. Certainly, you have seen this dynamic at play in your own life and in the lives of people you love.

There are some commonsense reasons why stress contributes to depression. When we are stressed, we may be tempted to abandon healthy habits we typically follow. Financial stress, for example, can lead to working long hours, skipping exercise, losing sleep due to worry, or eating fast food in the car on the way home from a late night at the office. When we forfeit proper exercise, sleep, and nutrition, we abandon three of our most powerful defenses against depression . . . and we lose three potent coping strategies for managing stress.

What's more, stress can also prompt us to seek temporary relief in unhealthy habits that create *more* stress in the long run. Turning to alcohol, comfort food, or overspending might provide temporary relief and distraction, but these things will complicate our lives and add to our stress over time.

But there's much more to this dynamic than the idea that stress tempts us to abandon good habits and pursue bad ones. Science tells us that when we experience stress—particularly ongoing, chronic stress like Kelley endured—it triggers processes within our bodies that are conducive to depression, even years after the stress or trauma occurred. Researchers are beginning to identify what these bodily processes are. What they are discovering is not only fascinating but also holds the possibility of alleviating the suffering of many people struggling with depression.

George Slavich and Michael Irwin, associated with UCLA's Cousins Center for Psychoneuroimmunology and Department of Psychiatry and Biobehavioral Sciences, began their quest for answers by asking the following questions:

- How does stress ramp up internal biological processes that evoke depression?
- Why is depression often accompanied by certain physical complaints, conditions, and diseases?
- Why are people with a history of early life stress at a greater risk for depression?

After analyzing more than 450 research papers, reviews, and studies on stress and depression, here's what Drs. Slavich and Irwin say is happening.

The body responds to different threats in different ways. For example, when physical injury or infection has occurred, localized inflammation is the body's signal for help. When skin or tissues are damaged, chemicals are released that increase blood flow to the area and also attract white blood cells to fight pathogens. In other words, inflammation is helping your immune system do its job.

But prolonged stress—especially stress related to interpersonal loss or rejection—triggers something called adaptive immunity, which not only increases inflammation at the sites of past trauma but also increases systemic inflammation throughout the entire body. And that's where the real problem lies.

Chronic, systemic inflammation has been linked to a variety of serious diseases, including "asthma, arthritis, diabetes, obesity, atherosclerosis, certain cancers, and Alzheimer's disease" . . . and, of course, depression.[1]

Professors at Rice University reviewed two hundred studies on depression and found that depression and inflammation are intertwined, feeding off each other:

This bidirectional loop, in which depression facilitates inflammatory responses and inflammation promotes depression, has clear health consequences. Heightened inflammation characterizes a number of disorders and systemic diseases, including cardiovascular disease, diabetes, metabolic syndrome, rheumatoid arthritis, asthma, multiple sclerosis, chronic pain, and psoriasis; each of these also features an elevated risk for depression.[2]

Furthermore, depression caused by chronic inflammation is resistant to traditional interventions (although it does respond to yoga, biofeedback, meditation, and exercise).

Stress Is on the Rise

The link between prolonged stress, systemic inflammation, and major depression isn't exactly good news, particularly since the amount of stress we experience today is, according to the American Psychological Association (APA), becoming a public health crisis. In fact, APA CEO Norman Anderson, PhD, says, "America is at a critical crossroads when it comes to stress and our health."[3]

What's stressing us out? Money and work rank as the two top stressors, with family responsibilities coming in third. Stress levels also seem higher the younger we are, with millennials reporting the highest average levels of stress (6.0 out of 10).[4]

Exacerbating the situation is that advances and innovations originally promising to relieve our stress—computers, smartphones, and the Internet, for example—appear simply to add to feelings of being overwhelmed. Here's what business and technology expert Bernard Marr has to say regarding why technology escalates our stress:

Data, data everywhere. Our brains are being expected to cope with data flowing into them from all directions as our computers, smart phones and connected devices constantly beep, flash and bombard us with information. . . . Put simply, the digital technology has evolved at a far quicker rate than the physical evolution of the brains we use to decipher and put it to use. Our brains aren't built to cope with the ever increasing volumes of data we are trying to cram into them—and this is leading to brain malfunction in the form of stress.[5]

Even something as seemingly innocuous as checking e-mail can add to our stress. Gloria Mark, a researcher at the University of California at Irvine, made interesting discoveries about e-mail stress when she conducted a study of a group of US Army civilian employees. After giving the test subjects heart rate monitors, she measured what happened when they eliminated e-mail from their lives for five days.

After the completion of their e-mail fast, employees' heart rate monitors showed that stress levels had decreased. Participants also reported that they felt more in control of their working lives and that productivity had improved.[6]

And what is the impact of all this stress? Studies are showing an increase in the number of people who report feeling nervous, anxious, depressed, sad, worried, irritable, or angry over previous years.[7] While this is not good news, it does give us a place to begin. It gives us hope that, by managing our stress (and inflammation), we can decrease depression and create a positive difference in our mood.

Take Control of What You Can Control

When our team of experts meets with clients every week, they are reminded that feeling stressed and overwhelmed by the demands of life is a common denominator. Not everything that causes us stress can be eliminated—nor should it be. Low-level stress stimulates the brain to boost productivity and concentration. It can also be a big motivator to make changes, solve problems, or accomplish goals that make us better human beings and create improvements in our lives.

In addition, many sources of stress are simply beyond our control. Sometimes things happen that we could not have foreseen or avoided, such as changes in the economy, an employer declaring bankruptcy, an accident or illness, or even the decisions of other people that leave us gravely affected.

That said, there are still plenty of stressors in our lives over which we do have control. Indeed, the elimination of stressors in this category will not only improve our lives but will also leave us healthier and happier. We are often tempted to complain about what we cannot control without ever making an effort to change or manage what we can control.

These controllable factors are the very things we ask clients to focus on, and you should focus on them in your life too. Here are seven stress-management strategies you should begin practicing immediately.

Stop Procrastinating

This is a simple (though not easy) place to start. It's safe to say we all procrastinate sometimes, and for some people, procrastination is a way of life. Whether you are an occasional procrastinator or a serial procrastinator, your delays and avoidance amp up your stress levels. Naturally, the more you procrastinate, the more stressed you become.

Chances are, at this very moment, there is something in your life that is making you feel anxious . . . not because you can't change it but because you are putting off doing what you need to do to resolve that source of stress once and for all.

Why do we procrastinate in the first place? Procrastination experts Joseph Ferrari, PhD, and Timothy Pychyl, PhD, say there are three types of procrastinators:

- "thrill-seekers," who get a rush out of waiting to the last minute
- "avoiders," who see procrastination as a way of sidestepping something unpleasant, like criticism or failure or even the unwanted pressure of success
- "decisional procrastinators," who struggle to make a decision and who thus may feel absolved of responsibility for how life unfolds[8]

Think back on the experiences of Kelley, whom I told you about earlier. The stress she experienced over the course of two decades came from a variety of sources, both within her control and beyond it. For example, while Kelley could not control her ex-husband's decision to renege on child support, she was in control of how long she waited before taking legal action. Kelley's procrastination was driven by her desire to avoid conflict, and it multiplied her stress many times over before she finally took action and resolved the problem.

Limit Your Commitments

Something else that is largely within your control to manage is how overcommitted you are. Granted, sometimes situations impose themselves on our lives and schedules, and we can find ourselves overwhelmed as a result. If we're not careful, we can grow accustomed to the feeling and continue to live in a familiar state of overload by never learning to say no.

Protecting your time from overcommitments that are within your control to refuse may not be easy, but it's arguably one of the most effective things you can do to reduce the stress in your life.

Forgo Temporary Escapes That Increase Your Stress

When we are stressed, it's tempting to turn to excessive eating, spending, or alcohol consumption. That's because we want to do something to change our mood! Of course, the list of unhelpful and unhealthy escapes could go on and on. Legal and illegal substance abuse, gambling, pornography, and infidelities may help us temporarily forget about the stress of our lives but will eventually leave us even more stressed—and depressed—than ever.

I'm not saying that finding ways to escape stress is a bad thing. In fact, taking a mental and emotional break from whatever is making you feel overwhelmed is a powerful tool that can improve how you cope, transform your perspective, and even help you identify long-term solutions. But being intentional about *how* we escape is critical, and what we choose can determine not only how long we stay stressed but how much damage we sustain in the process.

Embrace Healthy Escapes

What are some examples of healthy mini-vacations? An escape could be as simple as spending an hour with an enjoyable book in a backyard hammock or as elaborate as planning a trip to a bed-and-breakfast in another state.

You can also take an hour and try something brand new. For example, drive around a part of town you're unacquainted with until you find an unfamiliar coffee shop, go inside, and order something you've never tried before.

Plan a staycation and go camping in your backyard. Spend an afternoon at a local zoo or art museum. Visit a tourist attraction in your city that you've never been to before. Taking a walk in nature is an escape that is good for your body, your emotions, and your brain. Watching a favorite comedy is another escape that won't complicate your life or add to your stress after the credits roll.

Finally, you can cultivate healthy habits that you can practice when you feel stressed (instead of turning to unhealthy habits like bingeing on comfort food). One of our clients bought a mini trampoline and placed it in a corner of her kitchen. Because stress usually sends her to the pantry, she wanted a healthier alternative where she would be sure to see it. She is trying to be intentional about replacing her chocolate habit with the much healthier habit of bouncing lightly on her rebounder for five minutes whenever she starts to feel overwhelmed.

A word of caution and challenge on this point: depressed people usually do not want to embrace healthy escapes. They don't feel like it. These pursuits seem pointless or contrived or like too much work. Set aside justifications for doing nothing. Summon up any energy and motivation you can . . . and just do it!

Put an End to Isolation and Withdrawal

When we're stressed, it's tempting to isolate. When we're already feeling overwhelmed, the last thing we want to do is expend the energy to drive to an event, have someone over, or connect with a friend after work. And yet study after study shows that supportive relationships are huge factors when it comes to improving how we experience and process stress. In fact, loneliness is linked not only to depression but also to health problems including high blood pressure, cardiovascular disease, cancer, and cognitive decline.

It's worth noting here that involvement in a faith community may help in this regard. Studies have shown that people who are involved in faith communities tend to have lower levels of anxiety and stress. People who experience their faith with a supportive community are not only connecting with like-minded people, but they also feel more connected to God.

Therese Borchard, the founder of Project Hope & Beyond, an online community for people with depression and other mood disorders, writes,

> Religion and faith provide social support, a consistent
> element of happiness and good health. Regular churchgoers
> not only get support from their community, but they also

GIVE support to others, and the altruistic activity promotes better health. . . .

Faith attaches meaning to events. It gives folks hope, the ultimate stress reducer. Hope, doctors say, is about the best thing you can do for your body. It's better than a placebo.[9]

Guard Your Thoughts

Sometimes the source of our pain and stress can be found in our own thoughts. Ruminating on negative or painful experiences, refusing to forgive, or practicing a perennially negative outlook on life can create ongoing stress. What's more, because the source of this chronic stress isn't anything external that you can point to, it can be hard to identify and change.

We all have an inner voice constantly blabbering about our faults, failures, inadequacies, and unfortunate experiences. But did you know that you control the on/off switch for that voice? It may have had its own way for so long that you'll have to work to get the controls back. But you can. Refuse to sit still for self-inflicted verbal beatings any longer, and dam the flow of negative messages coming into your brain. Replace them with positive affirmations. Accept your shortcomings and celebrate your strengths. Refuse to ruminate about past hurts, and redirect your thoughts to uplifting memories. You will take a big step toward overcoming stress by recognizing the crucial role of thoughts and self-talk in creating your life.

Try this experiment: tonight before bed, set aside a few minutes to ponder and evaluate the quality of your thoughts throughout the day. Were they generally positive and productive? Critical and judgmental? Then think of some specific ways you can harness your thoughts and make them an ally, not an enemy, of your well-being. For instance, repeat to yourself the phrase "My thoughts will change as I create and plan—and I will feel more and more hope!"

Take Care of Your Body

One of the best things you can do to handle the stresses of life is to fortify your health and body. Eating right, getting enough sleep, and exercising regularly relieve feelings of stress and anxiety, improve your mood, and energize your body, brain, and emotions.

A major study, for example, tracked more than a million individuals to examine the association between exercise and mental health difficulties. Individuals who exercised consistently reported significantly fewer days of poor mental health in the past month than individuals who did not exercise but were otherwise matched for several physical and sociodemographic characteristics. All exercise types were associated with a lower mental health burden.[10]

We will look more closely at physical factors that affect depression in part 3.

It's impossible to eliminate all stress from your life. Managing stress well, thankfully, is another story. How much stress you experience—and how you respond when you experience that stress—is something over which you have more control than you may realize.

By keeping in mind these seven stress-busting strategies, you are taking an important step in improving the quality of your life as well as reducing a significant contributor to major depressive disorder.

Your Personal Action Plan

Reducing the stress in your life is not a one-time action but a series of lifestyle choices and intentional decisions. It's not something you figure out once but an attitude and a mind-set to be embraced now and for years to come.

What's the best way to get started? Begin by identifying some of the major stressors in your life. The following steps will help you begin the process.

1. **Identify key stressors.** Make a list of the factors in your life that are contributing to your stress. If possible, group these stressors into the categories we examined in this chapter:

   - stressors you might be able to eliminate if you stopped procrastinating
   - overcommitment issues
   - unhealthy habits you use to escape or avoid dealing with issues in a healthy manner
   - stress in your life that is causing, or is caused by, isolation
   - unhealthy ways of thinking that are adding to your stress
   - ways you are mistreating or neglecting your body

2. **Create an action plan to incorporate some of the strategies discussed in this chapter.** Trying to make immediate changes in all seven areas examined in this chapter will only add to your stress. Instead, identify two or three areas where you would like to incorporate changes and address those. Next month, incorporate a few additional changes, and so on.

3. **Identify a partner for accountability, encouragement, and company.** You're not the only one who is stressed. Chances are that you have friends who also would like to handle stress better. Ask someone you know to join you on this journey. Brainstorm, engage in fun stress-busting activities, hold each other accountable, and celebrate each other's successes together.

4. **When you mess up, don't stress about it.** As you are putting your plan into action, making new choices that will empower

you to handle stress better, there will be days when you fall back into old habits. Whether you binge on comfort food, say yes to too many commitments, stay up half the night watching mindless TV shows, or put off doing what you need to do to solve a stressful problem in your life, don't worry about it. Forgive yourself. Let it go. Move on.

5. **Celebrate your successes.** As you experience successes in your efforts to reduce the stress in your life, stop and savor the moment. Journal about the milestones in your journey—discovering a healthier way of seeing things, letting go of a grudge, improving your diet, beginning a workout program, getting to bed earlier, or tackling problems sooner rather than later.

CHAPTER 5

A Hard Look at Hard Issues

Uncovering Hidden Addictions Can Set You Free

Imagine you've planned a long sailing voyage. You've spent months preparing yourself and your boat. You've learned all you can about navigating through whatever the ocean throws at you. You've mapped the course you'll take and studied every available nautical chart for underwater hazards and currents. You've learned to recognize the signs of stormy weather approaching. The galley is provisioned, and the rigging on deck is checked and double-checked.

The day of departure arrives. You are as ready as you'll ever be for the great adventure ahead. The sun is shining and the wind is perfect, so you hoist the sails at last, look expectantly to the horizon, and go . . . nowhere.

That's because, after all your hard work and everything you've invested, you've neglected one very important detail: you forgot to raise the anchor. It is still firmly stuck in the mud, hidden under twenty feet of water, doing exactly what anchors do best—keeping you firmly in place.

This analogy often seems silly to people at first glance. After all, what sailor worth her salt would forget such an important step? But you'd be surprised how often the people who seek treatment for depression make exactly this mistake.

The journey they hope to make is not across the ocean; it's in search of a new life, free of depression and anxiety. Initially, they do the hard work addressed in the rest of this book: changing what they eat, improving their sleep habits, eliminating environmental toxins, addressing emotional baggage, and even forgiving those who have harmed them in some way—all the things that make up our whole-person treatment model. But at the end of the day, none of that is enough to set them free from depression, because something extraordinarily dense and heavy keeps them stuck in the mud.

They are tethered to the anchor of *addiction*.

This is so common, in fact, that at any given time as many as 40 percent of people at our mental health clinic seeking help with depression are concurrently enrolled in another of our major treatment programs—addiction rehab. In some ways, these people are the lucky ones, because their dependence on drugs or alcohol or both has become so apparent that they can no longer deny the obvious need for help.

At the other end of the spectrum, however, are people whose addictions are easier to hide—even from themselves. They have become dependent on behaviors that are legal and often considered "normal" in modern society and therefore harmless. Don't be fooled, though. These behaviors are just as heavy and just as likely to prevent you from making headway on your journey to healing.

Other People Are Addicts, Not Me

Addiction is a word that covers a lot of ground—everything from debilitating drug or alcohol use to out-of-control gambling. But in all cases, the working definition of addiction is the same: *continued compulsive substance use or behavior despite harmful consequences.*

To the person who is not addicted, that concept seems simple enough. If an action repeatedly has an adverse effect on your life but you can't or won't stop, then you are most likely addicted. That logic is easy to apply to others, yet few things are harder to recognize in ourselves than addiction.

It's not difficult to see why. The word *addict* is among the most stigmatized in the English language. Thanks to media-driven stereo-types, it conjures images of people who have lost all ability to function in society. We've convinced ourselves that addicts live in abandoned buildings or alleyways and spend their days begging or stealing for their next "fix." Those people certainly exist and are in great need of our help and compassion. But they form only a tiny fraction of the number of people whose lives are negatively affected by some com-pulsive need they can't control, whether physical or behavioral. The hard truth is, anyone can become addicted.

Surveys clearly back that up. According to the National Survey on Drug Use and Health, "approximately 21.5 million people aged 12 or older in 2014 had a substance use disorder (SUD) in the past year, including 17.0 million people with an alcohol use disorder, 7.1 mil-lion with an illicit drug use disorder, and 2.6 million who had both an alcohol use and an illicit drug use disorder."[1]

As stunning as those numbers sound, they include only people whose substance use rises to the clinical definition of a "disorder." Plus, the figures do not include the abuse of legal prescription drugs, a growing and deadly crisis in the United States, or other substances like tobacco, sugar, and caffeine, which would add many more mil-lions to the total. Furthermore, they don't begin to count the portion of the population trapped in compulsive behaviors such as gam-bling, shopping, video games, and so on, which the mental health community has only just begun to suspect are addictions in the truest sense of the word.

Here's the point: if you are struggling to overcome depression and are also addicted to a harmful substance or behavior, you are not alone. And you are not flawed or inferior. Addiction is not a character defect. It is not a moral failure or a sign of weakness. It is a sign of pain. It is an attempt to meet a legitimate need in yourself that has, until now, gone unacknowledged and unmet. We'll return to that idea later in the chapter, but for now it's also important to face a hard truth: *you are going nowhere in your search for lasting freedom from depression while an addiction weighs you down.*

The fact is, an addiction of any kind will alter your mood, and that is precisely what people want when they are feeling depressed. Since compulsive involvement with addictive substance or activity usually brings temporary relief, pleasure, or even bliss, it's not surprising that the depressed individual returns to this behavior again and again. Quite often, the person pursues the harmful habit more intensely and more frequently in order to achieve the same mood elevation and sense of relief.

Meanwhile, compulsive behaviors do nothing to address the real causes of depression. In fact, they only mask and distract from them. One of the themes of this book is that depression almost never goes away on its own. What's more, depression typically gets worse if a person doesn't explore the root causes, and especially if habits and patterns persist that contribute to mood imbalance.

All this is why facing and overcoming addiction of any kind is absolutely necessary to healing depression.

What's It Got to Do with Depression?

That's a question a lot of people ask when we first bring up the issue of addiction in treatment. The link is more obvious when people have developed a serious dependence on illicit drugs or alcohol. Those folks generally must undergo three to five days of intense, medically supervised detox before anything else can begin. But when it comes to other, less obvious compulsive behaviors, we often hear objections like these:

"I need those ten cups of coffee in the morning *because* I'm depressed, not the other way around." This person couldn't see that caffeine had left them chronically dehydrated and had leached essential vitamins out of their system, seriously interfering with healthy mood regulation.

"Time on the Internet takes my mind off things when nothing else will." Maybe, but it also increases social isolation, inhibits healthy exercise and eating habits, and promotes distraction and the fear of missing out if you step away even for a moment—all of which work against your recovery.

"Everyone shops—it's totally normal. I like nice things, so leave me alone about it." And yet excessive and compulsive spending leads directly to negative consequences in your financial well-being and frequently in your relationships as well, providing ample reasons to feel depressed.

In fact, a predictable sequence of actions and feelings come along with addiction, links in the chain of the anchor keeping you stuck in depression. Here's how it works:

Secrecy. Most people know without being told when their behavior or substance use begins to tip out of balance. Perhaps they don't yet see a problem in it, but they sense that others will not understand and will disapprove of their actions. So they hide them. No matter how we try to convince ourselves otherwise, we hide only what we are ashamed of, and so a low-level conflict begins within us.

Deception. Before long, the need to hide our secret forces us to lie, usually to people who care about us. We might be able to justify having personal secrets, but everyone knows that deceiving people close to us is toxic to healthy relationships. Which leads to heightened . . .

Shame and guilt. If depression were a rocket, then these two would be the fuel. They can enter our thinking from many directions, but when they arise because we're harboring a secret addiction, one we lie to keep hidden, then shame and guilt lead directly to feeling powerless, worthless, and unlovable—all the hallmarks of entrenched depression.

Finally, the reflexive response of someone in the grip of growing addiction and depression is this:

Further self-medication. And just like that, the cycle of secrecy, deception, shame, and guilt—all driving us into depression—starts over again, this time in a higher gear.

What does addiction have to do with depression? *Everything.*

All Addictions Are Created Equal

We've already mentioned the differences between addiction to a substance and addiction to other types of behaviors. The latter is referred to in the mental health profession as "process addictions" or "soft addictions."

What we haven't yet discussed is how these two classes of addictions are *alike*. Recent research has revealed a startling fact: the human brain reacts in very similar ways to substance and process addictions, in some cases appearing to be almost identical in brain scans. For example, a 2010 study found that pathological gamblers and those addicted to substances "share many clinical, phenomenological, and biological features."[2]

The point is, as research continues to confirm findings like these, there is less reason than ever to treat "process addictions" any less seriously than substance addictions. Both can create negative outcomes in the lives of addicts, including the onset and deepening severity of depression. To underscore the danger, the National Council on Problem Gambling reported in 1997 that as many as one in five pathological gamblers had attempted suicide and that suicide rates among gamblers were the highest of any addictive disorder, substances included.[3]

The following is a roundup of dependencies, arranged in broad categories, that we commonly see in people who seek treatment for depression at our clinic. Keep in mind, however, that addictions come in many variations. If you recognize yourself in these brief descriptions, rest assured the purpose is not to shame you or burden you with yet another mountain to climb. It is to help you free yourself of everything keeping you chained to depression—by leading you to step one: recognizing there could be a problem that needs your attention.

Substances

The United States Surgeon General estimates that one in seven Americans will develop a substance abuse disorder at some point during their lifetime.[4]

ALCOHOL

It should come as no surprise that alcohol abuse is a massive problem worldwide. Alcohol abuse disorder can be diagnosed in nearly 5 percent of the population worldwide (240 million people).[5] In the United States, one in eight (12.7 percent) "meets diagnostic criteria for alcohol use disorder."[6] Not only is alcohol use legal for adults, but it is also widely accepted as a normal part of everyday life. Drinking is how we celebrate good days and commiserate over bad ones. It's easy to see how its use can spin out of control, especially among people who are looking for a way to numb the pain of toxic emotions like shame, guilt, fear, and anger.

Alcohol *is* a depressant. Addiction not only invites myriad negative consequences into a person's life, but over time it also rewires the brain so that having a drink is necessary just to feel normal.

TOBACCO

One of the most addictive substances known, nicotine is a stimulant that triggers a rush of adrenaline in the bloodstream, along with dopamine, sometimes called the brain's "happy chemical" because of its association with pleasure and reward.

However, research indicates a direct link between smoking and depression, in part because nicotine disrupts mood control by altering the brain's natural ability to regulate these chemicals.[7] That's on top of other well-documented negative health effects of prolonged tobacco use.

PRESCRIPTION MEDICATION

The misuse of legally prescribed medication is nothing new. However, a flood of cheap and accessible opioid painkillers in the United States has made the problem many orders of magnitude worse. Overdose numbers justify naming this an "epidemic." Mike Stobbe, a medical writer for the Associated Press, reported in 2017 that

> there were fewer than 3,000 overdose deaths in 1970, when a heroin epidemic was raging in U.S. cities. There were fewer than 5,000 recorded in 1988, around the height of the crack epidemic. More than 64,000 Americans died from drug overdoses [in 2016], according to the U.S. Centers for Disease Control and Prevention.[8]

That's an increase of more than tenfold, and the vast majority of those deaths were caused by opioid drugs. Still, these numbers don't begin to quantify the devastation opioid addiction causes well before overdose claims a person's life.

ILLICIT DRUGS

One side effect of the prescription opioid epidemic is to drive people to use heroin once they can no longer obtain legal substances like oxycodone. To make matters worse—and exponentially more lethal—chemists have synthesized a new opioid painkiller called fentanyl. It is up to a hundred times more potent than morphine and thirty to fifty times more potent than heroin, according to the US Drug Enforcement Administration.[9]

The list of other illicit drugs that are addictive is long and growing, including cocaine, methamphetamines, hallucinogens, tranquilizers, stimulants, and marijuana.

FOODS: CAFFEINE, SUGAR, AND FAT

Often overlooked in the discussion of addictive and potentially harmful substances are those found in our food. As we've already seen, addiction to caffeine can cause serious physical harm and contribute directly to depression.

The same can be said of sugar and fat, common ingredients in a wide range of processed foods, not just the obvious ones. Studies have shown a direct link between sugar intake and disruption to mood regulation.[10]

Processes

Because the mental health research community has only just begun the systematic study of process addictions, comprehensive statistics are difficult to come by. However, plenty of evidence exists that Americans are increasingly trapped in a wide range of compulsive behaviors with significant adverse impacts on their lives. These include the following:

EATING

As we've seen, foods that are high in sugar and fat (as nearly all fast food is) act on the brain's pleasure and reward centers, triggering the release of dopamine. Binge eating can develop when we use food as a source of comfort and reward. In addition to negative health effects, food addiction leaves a person feeling powerless and guilty, emotions that are directly related to depression.

INTERNET

We've already seen in chapter 3 the various ways technology can cause and exacerbate depression. However, some people mistakenly think if they aren't gambling online or compulsively watching pornography or obsessively checking social media accounts, they don't have a problem with the Internet. In fact, simply being online for hours at a time, no matter what sites you visit, can be addictive and a source of trouble for anyone struggling with depression.

SOCIAL MEDIA

The compulsive need to engage with social media platforms is a growing problem worldwide. The fear of missing out and being left behind drives people to prioritize staying connected over other obligations and relationships—and even their day-to-day well-being.

VIDEO GAMES

There is disagreement among researchers whether compulsive gaming rises to the clinical definition of an addiction. But in my experience, that's an argument over academic details when the real-world truth is obvious: chronic and compulsive video game playing heightens social isolation and mood swings while inhibiting full engagement in other life relationships and responsibilities.[11]

PORNOGRAPHY/SEX

Compulsive sexual behavior has many manifestations, but perhaps the most addictive of them is the excessive use of pornography. It affects the same neurological pleasure and reward mechanisms we've already discussed and can negatively influence a person's social relationships and self-esteem.[12]

RELATIONSHIPS/LOVE

Codependency is difficult to define, but it is sometimes referred to as "relationship addiction" because it involves excessive emotional or psychological reliance on another person, typically someone with significant needs of their own. Codependency is common among people struggling with mental health issues because it usually arises from unresolved childhood trauma and deep feelings of worthlessness, the very things that fuel depression.

SHOPPING

Compulsive buying is a disorder recognized by mental health professionals, thought to have roots in a poorly regulated search for validation and identity through material purchases, among other causes. Whatever the origin, an addiction to shopping frequently results in adverse consequences—in the areas of financial well-being, relationships, depression, and anxiety.

GAMBLING

Based on research we've already discussed, gambling is the only behavior formally recognized as an addiction in the *Diagnostic and Statistical Manual of Mental Disorders*. It leads to a host of negative outcomes, including severe depression.[13]

EXERCISE

In psychological parlance called "Body Dysmorphic Disorder," this condition is an excellent example of an otherwise healthy behavior that can spin out of control and lead to adverse life consequences. A person addicted to exercise will spend too much time at the activity, to the detriment of their professional and personal life; will exercise to the point of physical harm; and may experience withdrawal anxiety when their routine is interrupted.

ANGER/CONTROL

In the next chapter, we will talk at length about how unresolved toxic emotions—anger, fear, and guilt—contribute to depression. But the unregulated expression of anger, in outbursts of rage and even physical violence, can become a compulsive behavior beyond a person's ability to manage. For that person, losing control becomes the only way to get relief from runaway emotion. That leads directly to the other two toxic emotions: fear of losing relationships and guilt at being unable to improve. Combined, these form the perfect recipe for depression.

Confronting Addiction, Healing Depression

That's a daunting list of addictive substances and behaviors. There is no point in pretending that tackling one or more of these in yourself will be easy, quick, or simple. It will take committed focus and effort. But the good news is, dealing with your addictions will immediately pay off in every area of your life—including mental health. The short-term benefit of clinging to compulsive behavior pales in comparison to the priceless treasure of freedom, health, and well-being.

So, where do you start? With detox.

No matter what substance or behavior has you trapped in dependency, the first step will always be to break its immediate power over you. That means accepting the difficult realities of withdrawal because you are determined to escape the much worse consequences of inaction. Be prepared for your body and mind to rebel, because they are, initially, just as determined to stay stuck in the mud. But it's a battle you can win—one you *must* win to progress in your quest for freedom from depression.

After a period of time, your mind will begin to clear and you can use the following questions to recover your perspective and empower you to make new choices.

1. **Am I addicted?** If your continued behavior clearly has resulted in negative outcomes in your life and you keep doing it anyway, then there is no other conclusion: you are addicted. Facing that is the only way you'll find the strength to do what must be done to be free. If you still believe you can stop anytime you want, ask yourself, *Why haven't I?*

2. **What need is this behavior meeting?** Ask yourself, *What do I feel before and after I indulge in this behavior, and what clues are in those feelings that help me better understand my unmet needs?*

3. **What am I avoiding with this behavior?** A person who routinely drinks to excess may be running from past traumas or current conflicts they'd rather not face. The distraction of the Internet may be a convenient way to avoid admitting you are not happy in your job or relationship and to sidestep your fear of change. However you answer this question, it is valuable information because it marks the spot where you must dig to unearth more pieces to the puzzle of lasting healing.

4. **How can I meet this need differently?** Once you know what longing you are trying to fulfill, it's easier to see that there are other healthier ways to get there. If pornography is masking the fact that you feel lonely and unlovable and if what you truly need is genuine human connection, then turning off the computer is step one in a campaign to put yourself in a position to meet real people. That may take time, and it may involve the work of self-improvement, but it is a positive path with real potential to meet your need in a way that continued addiction never will.

In the old days of tall sailing ships, raising the anchor was hard work. It took a team of sailors working together at the capstan to lift the monstrous thing out of the muck, one heavy link of chain at a time, and stow it away. But after the sweating and exertion were done, a whole new world awaited.

Your Personal Action Plan

As we have explored in the previous pages, the presence of an addiction significantly contributes to depression . . . and depression frequently contributes to the downward spiral of addiction. Even as we look squarely at this disturbing dilemma, let's not lose sight of an inspiring fact: each year, countless people address their addictive behaviors and make substantial progress in overcoming them. And you can too! Begin your journey toward healing with these steps:

1. **Get real.** You've lived in secrecy and behind a screen of lies for so long that you may feel there's no way back. How can you come clean now after so much time? Rest assured that, even now, people who care about you would rather hear the truth, however painful, than go on struggling with a vague suspicion that something is not right. Getting secrets out of the closet and into the light is remarkably liberating for everyone involved. Freed of that burden, you'll have more energy and motivation to complete the work you've started and beat addiction and depression for good.

2. **Get help.** It's no accident that every community in America has a wide range of thriving recovery programs available for every addiction you can name. They exist and persist because people exactly like you have discovered an undeniable fact: they can't succeed alone. Help can also come in the form

of professional counseling, trusted friends and family, and involvement in faith communities.

3. **Get active.** Wanting to recover is not enough. Healing is something you *do*, not passively receive. Make a list of steps you can take right now to be free. Guard against populating your plan with only low-hanging fruit. Include items that scare you, that you think are impossible—and do them anyway.

4. **Get out.** If shopping is your compulsion, get out of the mall. If it's drinking, get out of the bar. In other words, the thing that has you trapped exists in a particular environment, associated with a known group of people, at certain times of day, and under predictable circumstances. Make a list of what those are, and then remove yourself from them.

5. **Get accountable.** Your brain is a smooth talker, especially when in search of a dopamine fix. Its justifications seem reasonable and harmless enough when confined to your private, inner dialogue. But speak them out loud to someone who has agreed to help you make good choices, and those arguments become much easier to see for what they are.

PART 2

Soul

CHAPTER 6

The Three Deadly Emotions

How Unresolved Anger, Guilt, and
Fear Undermine Healing

One look at Andrew was all it took to see he was ready to give up hope for a better future. Perhaps he had done so already, since it hadn't been his choice to seek help for his depression. He had finally sought counsel only because his wife drew a line in the sand of their marriage and insisted. She wasn't blaming or demanding; she was frightened and confused, like so many people who are dealing with a loved one's depression.

When I asked Andrew to describe his struggles, he answered, "Insomnia. If I could just get a good night's sleep, everything would be fine." Yet the more we talked about the state of his life and his feelings about it, the clearer it became that Andrew was severely depressed. Insomnia was only one of several common indicators—both a symptom and a source of his distress.

Andrew was employed as a firefighter, a job he once enjoyed. Now, it was all he could do to get out of bed each day, let alone climb tall ladders and hoist heavy hoses. For the first time in his life, he suffered migraine headaches that were increasing in frequency and severity. Meals at the station were mostly healthy fare, but on his days off Andrew ate fast food, microwave dinners, and sugary snacks. He stopped going to the gym. As a result, he was rapidly gaining enough weight to draw the attention of his chief and fellow firefighters—reinforcing his growing dread of being at work. He knew his deteriorating physical condition might eventually jeopardize his job, but he couldn't muster the energy or resolve to take action. His off-duty alcohol consumption went from one beer with dinner to a six-pack or more every night.

Andrew's family physician noticed these changes and had his suspicions confirmed when Andrew scored alarmingly high on a patient survey designed to assess mental health in the primary care setting. The doctor suggested antidepressant medication, which Andrew immediately rejected, offended by the idea he needed a "crutch" to carry him through. The doctor persisted and arranged an appointment for Andrew at a nearby mental health clinic. He didn't show.

On a hunch, I asked Andrew if he'd recently experienced something particularly traumatic at work. Firefighters are often the first on the scene of horrific accidents or acts of violence, and it can be difficult for them to cope with what they experience at such times.

"No," was his curt reply.

Intuition told me to try again.

"Well, not recently," he said, grudgingly. "Not here."

"Where then?"

Andrew's reaction made it clear we were finally getting somewhere. His jaw muscles rippled as he clamped his mouth shut. His breathing became shallow and forced. His eyes darted around the room, often returning to the door—his only avenue of escape. For several moments we sat in silence, Andrew struggling to keep his composure.

"What happened to you, Andrew?" I asked gently.

Then the dam broke, and a torrent of emotion poured out of him. As soon as he answered the question of "where," then the "what" was obvious: Andrew had been a soldier in Afghanistan and lived through the unspeakable horrors of combat. He'd left the Marine Corps four years prior to our meeting, opting for firefighting after his honorable discharge from military service. Despite the passage of time, all that he had seen and done during two tours of duty in some of the roughest parts of war-torn Afghanistan was still fresh in his mind, as if it had happened only yesterday.

It was true that Andrew suffered from severe depression and exhibited several classic symptoms: loss of energy and motivation, feelings of worthlessness and despair, trouble sleeping, self-destructive behaviors like binge eating and misusing alcohol, and so on. But it was immediately apparent to me that something more fundamental lay at the root of Andrew's condition, a corrosive emotion that the medical profession has been slow to associate with depression, though thankfully, that is beginning to change.

If Andrew's condition had a geographic center, it was this: he was intensely *angry*.

In Afghanistan, Andrew had spent many months in a state of nearly perpetual danger. He had watched his friends die or suffer horrible wounds, young men far from their homes, just "trying to make the world a better place." He'd seen other people fall victim as well, some of whom were clearly enemy combatants, but many more whose only apparent crime was being in the wrong place at the wrong time. Worst of all, as a soldier, he had been required to commit violence of his own.

Thankfully, Andrew escaped physical injury while in the service, but that didn't mean he came home unscathed. He was angry at the world for being such a cruel and dangerous place, at the average complacent American who had "no idea what it's like out there," and for regrettable things he'd done that were just "part of the job." Most of all, he was angry at himself for surviving when others hadn't.

Once Andrew opened up about his traumatic past, it was not hard to see that anger was a major contributing factor in his depression. In fact, in my experience, unresolved anger and depression often travel together, one fanning the flames of the other until, if unchecked, the heat threatens to consume a person's life entirely.

There's plenty of scientific research to back up that statement. Study after study has shown a causative and reinforcing link between runaway anger and depression, among other negative health effects. But, as valuable as that realization is in helping to guide us toward lasting victory over depression, we can't stop there. Anger, you see, is only one part of a triad of feelings that are nearly inseparable and that together can form a slippery slope to deeper and deeper depression.

To uncover the other two, let's continue with Andrew's story.

The Terrible Triplets

When he returned to civilian life, Andrew's family and friends—especially his wife—were all understandably delighted to have him home. To them, it was cause for celebration, and he endured a series of "welcome back" parties that allowed little room for processing his true feelings. What he felt on the inside—fierce anger—did not match the expectations of others. So, to avoid disappointing or offending them, he suppressed his turmoil. Or tried to, at any rate.

We're all familiar with the saying "Where there's smoke, there's fire." But the reverse is just as true: when a fire is burning, it's impossible to hide it. There will be smoke. Things nearby will warp and wither in the heat. In Andrew's case, that meant the harder he tried to deny his anger, the more it flared up in unexpected ways. He was moody and harshly demanding with his wife for no apparent reason. He had no patience with coworkers and let them know it with frequent cutting remarks. He was prone to road rage at the slightest provocation and had lost all control on occasion, nearly crashing his car. Worst of all, these impulses were completely beyond his ability to manage. It was as if a hungry tiger lived inside him, prowling his life, looking for prey.

All of this frightened him. For Andrew, depression—succumbing to the anesthetic of feeling nothing at all—was preferable to living with his unpredictable anger day in and day out. In fact, it is common for people with unresolved anger, guilt, and fear to actively choose the relative emotional numbness of depression as a defense and escape.

And that's where the second of the three deadly emotions enters the picture: *guilt*.

On top of his anger, Andrew felt guilty for how he treated people. He expected better of himself and felt ashamed at being unable to live up to his expectations. Which led straight to the third emotion: *fear*.

Andrew became terrified that his experiences in war had left him hopelessly broken and in danger of losing everything he had clung to through the long months spent in harm's way—his wife, his family, and a future worth having. He also feared that his inability to find solid emotional footing was a sign that something was terribly wrong with him.

To make matters worse, these were not the only reasons Andrew had for feeling guilty and afraid. He was haunted by things he had done in the heat of combat or that he had stood by and watched others do. He tortured himself with the question, *What kind of person am I?* He was terrified of what others would think of him if they could see into his memories and read his thoughts.

Thus, anger, guilt, and fear formed a poisonous fog in Andrew's mind that contributed directly to—you guessed it—*depression*. It's not hard to see how a person in this circumstance might conclude:

I'm worthless.
Life is hopeless and not worth living.
I don't deserve to be happy and well.
Nobody could possibly love me.

Once someone is in that frame of mind, the downward spiral picks up speed. In Andrew's case, depression prompted unhealthy eating habits, which led to weight gain and deteriorating physical fitness. He started drinking too much, giving him extra reasons to be afraid of losing his wife and his job and for feeling guilty about his powerlessness—all of which points to deeper depression.

Prerequisite to Progress

In my decades of working with people desperate to overcome depression, I have learned that Andrew's story is not at all unusual. The three deadly emotions of anger, fear, and guilt—and their uncanny ability to fuel one another—are nearly always present to some degree in the hearts and minds of people suffering from depression. Clearly, not everyone has a story as dramatic as Andrew's, but that doesn't matter. The damage that anger, fear, and guilt can cause in your life is the same, no matter what ignites the fire to begin with. Here are just a few common sources of toxic anger I've seen:

- mistreatment (real or perceived) during childhood
- being unfairly denied promotion at work or deserved recognition in other contexts
- unresolved conflicts with family and friends
- infidelity and divorce
- illness and the sense of "why me?" injustice it can prompt
- financial misfortune
- grief at a painful loss that turns to bitterness
- general social injustice and "righteous rage"

Sadly, sometimes the traumas and offenses to which people cling are not even real but only imagined—like the woman who told me she was intensely depressed and angry for months after her sister failed to acknowledge her completion of graduate school, when in fact the postal service had lost a package containing a thoughtful and expensive gift.

Also, it's important to notice that everything on this list could just as easily be a source of guilt and fear instead. The interplay between these deadly emotions is like an ever-shifting kaleidoscope, each twisted shape blending into the next. For instance, change the circumstances, and anger at a spouse's infidelity becomes guilt for your own, or fear of possible unfaithfulness in the future. Perhaps anger is followed by the guilty feeling that a partner's infidelity is proof there is something desperately wrong with *you*, leading to the fear that you don't deserve to be happy again.

Can you see why thought patterns like these are so detrimental to your mental health? It is difficult to say which comes first, runaway deadly emotions or depression. But in any case, they have a proven and powerfully negative influence on one another. If you are prone to depression for other reasons, these toxic feelings will rob you of the natural resilience you need to keep or regain your balance.

Here's the important part for anyone struggling with depression: lasting healing is not possible when unexamined and untended anger, guilt, and fear smolder beneath the surface of your life. They will undermine any progress made on other fronts—such as nutrition, sleep, and exercise—and place a hard limit on what's possible. For this reason, while some traditional treatments for depression ignore these emotions, the whole-person model makes diffusing them a high priority, just as important as any other link in the chain of healing.

A Time for Everything

We won't come any closer to healing depression if we simply brand anger, guilt, and fear as undesirable and attempt to bury them away. Like many dangerous things, even emotions that can have such a deadly effect on mental and physical health may also play a positive role in our lives. There are two sides to every coin. In this case, the trick is in seeing the fundamental difference between the side of our emotions that leads to the darkness of depression and the side that is healthy and life giving.

The key to understanding lies in the word *power*.

The immediate result of runaway and deadly anger, guilt, and fear is not depression; it is a sense of *powerlessness*, the belief that you have no control over the circumstances of your life. Andrew was angry because he felt powerless to save his friends from harm. He felt powerless to stop the violence he'd been forced to participate in. He felt powerless to communicate his feelings to others who had not shared his experience of war. And it made him angry. He felt powerless over his rising sense of guilt and fear—and over his own detrimental behaviors as a result.

This is the soil in which depression grows.

Is it possible for those same emotions to lead to empowerment instead? Yes, it is. In fact, that's the purpose of proper and balanced emotions—even heated ones like anger, guilt, and fear. They are meant to guide us into thoughts and actions that make life better. Here's how.

Anger. There are times when anger is not only appropriate but also positively beneficial. That's because anger—like pain—is a signal that something is not right in our environment. Something important needs our attention. Anger motivates us to

- correct what needs correcting, in the world and in ourselves;
- set and keep personal boundaries;

- defend ourselves when threatened;
- stand up for others in need of help; and
- lend our voices to important issues in our communities.

Appropriate anger is the warning light on the dashboard of our lives alerting us to the need for action.

Guilt. There are two types of guilt—*self-correcting* and *self-loathing*. You might also call them true guilt (justified) and false guilt (unjustified). The first occurs naturally when you recognize you've made a mistake. It's a spontaneous emotional signal that you need to make amends and give thought to avoiding the same mistake in the future. For example, suppose you participate in a workplace conversation that unfairly tears down a coworker, possibly jeopardizing the person's standing within the organization. Later, you feel bad about your behavior, knowing it was not right. That sense of guilt is a sign of healthy self-correction. As a result, you might be moved to apologize to the target of gossip and set the record straight. At the very least, you are more likely to stand up for what's right the next time around.

It's obvious from its name that the second type of guilt—self-loathing—is the kind that contributes to depression. It may also be prompted by a particular incident, but rather than encouraging introspection and self-improvement, it results in a generalized feeling of unworthiness. That's not something we know how to correct, so it lingers and grows until it stops being about something we may have *done* and becomes a statement on *who we are*: worthless. Combine that with other common ingredients, and you've got a recipe for depression.

Fear. If you are walking alone through a darkened parking lot at night in a rough neighborhood, a dose of fear-induced adrenaline is a very helpful asset. It sharpens your senses and reflexes, preparing you to fight or flee, should it become necessary. It's what kept our ancestors alive back when the "neighborhood" was likely to be filled with hungry carnivores and pillaging enemies.

But what happens when fear (or anger or guilt) becomes a way of life—no longer a momentary response to specific dangers but a constant, low-level tension? In that case, these emotions have exactly the opposite effect, with all sorts of physical and emotional consequences—including depression. According to researchers at Mayo Clinic,

> the long-term activation of the stress-response system—
> and the subsequent overexposure to cortisol and other stress
> hormones—can disrupt almost all your body's processes.
> This puts you at increased risk of numerous health problems,
> including: anxiety, depression, digestive problems, headaches,
> heart disease, sleep problems, weight gain, memory and
> concentration impairment.[1]

Incidentally, the "stress-response system" surrounding fear releases the same neurochemicals as chronic anger does—adrenaline and cortisol. Research has shown that, while these two compounds are essential and beneficial in short bursts, chronic exposure produces significant disruption to your body's immune system, opening the door to all manner of secondary health problems. One of the most striking things about the above Mayo Clinic list is that it's full of conditions that mental-health professionals encounter with people who believe they are simply suffering from depression. In other words, depression never stands alone. It is always both the circular cause and the effect of numerous other factors—including letting the three deadly emotions go unresolved.

A Way Out and a Way Up

The good news is that your emotions do not have to dictate the direction of your life, including your struggle with depression. It is possible to keep your emotions in balance so that they empower you and don't encumber you. But how can we know the difference between healthy anger, guilt, and fear and the versions that have turned destructive?

The answer lies in the idea I introduced a moment ago: *empowerment*. If your anger is momentary and leaves you feeling determined to make some positive change in your life . . . and if guilt has opened your eyes to some area in your life in need of improvement . . . and if fear has alerted you to danger and given you the impulse you need to get out of harm's way—then your emotions have empowered you to be stronger, better, and wiser.

On the other hand, if your anger, guilt, and fear have left you feeling powerless over your life circumstances . . . if they have robbed you of hope or confidence in your ability to overcome . . . and if they have become an excuse for self-destructive behaviors and addictions—then you have become their slave.

The good news about overheated emotions is that you need not live as their hostage. It is possible to regain the upper hand over what you feel and why. It's understandable if your first reaction is to doubt that claim. Chances are you've been living with deadly anger, guilt, and fear for so long that they seem woven into your very personality. Don't despair! This is not true. With discipline and concentrated effort on your part—and with support from professionals and others in your life willing to help—you will see a dramatic change when you set out to tame your emotions.

That's the conclusion of Andrew's story. He committed to a whole-person treatment program that included dealing with the feelings he'd been trying so hard to deny. Within just a few months, his life looked very different than it did on the day he first walked into my office. He was sleeping again, had shed much of his extra weight, and best of all, had lost the shadow of hopelessness that had drained his life of joy and meaning.

Healing like this can be yours, too!

Your Personal Action Plan

As you set out to be free of depression, it's important to start with an honest look at how runaway feelings may be a large part of the problem and to be reassured that you are not simply stuck in emotional limbo. We'll look at a strategy for dealing with toxic emotions in the next chapter, but here are five ways to get going:

1. **Accept that anger, guilt, and fear may be making you ill (emotionally, physically, or both).** Research abounds on this subject. Educate yourself on the myriad negative effects that chronic toxic emotions have on your well-being. Take responsibility for the fact that these impacts are, to a large degree, self-inflicted—so long as you leave your emotions untended and unmended.

2. **Examine the source of your anger, guilt, and fear.** In your journal write, "I am angry because . . ." and write in as many reasons as you can. Don't try to filter your responses. Be honest and let them flow. Now do the same thing again: "I feel guilty because . . ." "I feel afraid because . . ." By the time you are done with this exercise, you'll have created an emotional map of the hot spots in your life—thoughts, beliefs, and memories that need your attention if you hope to be well.

3. **Be willing to let go and feel something else.** Sounds simple and easy, but it's not! This takes practice and persistence. The truth is, powerful emotions are addictive. Your body develops a strong dependence on the chemicals that flood your bloodstream in response to certain feelings. You cling to them because you receive a counterproductive "payoff" by letting them run free. So at this stage in your recovery, it's important to make a firm decision that you will confront this pattern of

behavior and replace it with something else. Again, open your journal and write, "I am tired of feeling angry (guilty, fearful) all the time because _____. I'd rather feel _____ instead."

4. **Give yourself and others permission to be "only" human.** A key source of runaway anger, guilt, and fear is trying to live up to standards that are unrealistic and expecting others to do the same. People are fallible, yourself included! As a person of faith, I am convinced that God loves us all and doesn't hold our failings against us. You'll take a major step in the direction of healing by following God's lead and lightening up on yourself and others.

5. **Seek out professional help.** When beginning the process of taming the bramble of old and thorny emotions in yourself, talk therapy and cognitive behavioral therapy (CBT) can provide exactly the tools you need to succeed. At The Center, we use a variation of CBT called dialectical behavioral therapy (DBT), which is a clear and cogent process for working through strong emotions, shifting them from harmful to helpful. Using these techniques or others, a compassionate counselor can show you all the ways your emotions have turned into maladapted behaviors and habits so that you are more able to choose another way to be.

CHAPTER 7

The Antidote for Toxic Emotions

Forgiveness Is the Remedy—
and a Relief for Depression

After reading the previous chapter and learning that anger, guilt, and fear could be poisoning your efforts to heal from depression, you may be thinking, *Now what? It's one thing to see my emotions for what they are but quite another to be free of them! You don't know what this feels like on the inside!*

Thankfully, the outlook is not as bleak as that, and the task not nearly as overwhelming. There is a proven antidote to toxic emotion—and a powerful tonic for regaining control over your health and well-being. However, like everything else on the road to healing depression for good, it's not a magic elixir you can ingest for instantaneous and miraculous relief. This cure will require tough choices, discipline, and commitment on your part. It will take courage to face the emotional dragons you've hidden away in your closet over the years and to dare to think differently about them. But it can be done! Proof lies in the millions of people who have gone before you and found freedom in the age-old practice of *forgiveness*.

Now, I am well aware that *forgiveness* is a loaded word for many people. It carries conflicting religious overtones or hints of pop culture sentimentalism many of us have learned to mistrust. The response I often get when I first bring it up with depressed clients is "You want me to do *what*?"

I respond, "Consider forgiving all those who have harmed you or caused you pain in your life."

"Are you kidding me?" they retort. "Just let them get away with treating me like that? Forget all about it? No way. Not going to happen."

This kind of resistance to the idea of forgiveness arises, in part, out of sheer force of habit. That is, the person has been nursing resentment, revenge fantasies, and simmering outrage for so long that it's difficult to imagine life without intense feelings. For many of us, anger, guilt, fear, and judgment are more than mere emotions. They've become an armored identity. We wonder who and what we'll be if we let go.

Well, we'll be better off, that's what—100 percent of the time.

In the Christian tradition, forgiveness is viewed as essential. I don't think that's intended as a spiritual obligation as much as it is practical advice for lifelong health and well-being—and healing grace when we need a little help overcoming depression.

Forgiveness is a blessing, not a burden. It's a source of the very peace you're looking for when pursuing lasting relief from depression. That's not just wishful thinking. It's amply supported by scientific research as well. In an article titled "Forgiveness: Your Health Depends on It," researchers at Johns Hopkins University states,

> The good news: Studies have found that the act of
> forgiveness can reap huge rewards for your health, lowering

the risk of heart attack; improving cholesterol levels and sleep; and reducing pain, blood pressure, and levels of anxiety, depression and stress. And research points to an increase in the forgiveness-health connection as you age.[1]

In a landmark meta-analysis of available research on the subject of forgiveness and mental health published in a volume called *Handbook of Forgiveness*, psychologists Loren Toussaint and Jon R. Webb discovered that nine recent studies had all concluded the same thing: forgiveness has a significant role to play in healing depression.[2]

"He Fouled Me!"

The 2003 film *Seabiscuit* illustrates the essential value of forgiveness in a brilliant scene involving a troubled racehorse jockey named Red Pollard (played by Tobey Maguire). The whole story is a study in learning to let go of the past and forgive in order to reclaim a better future.

In the film's version of events, Pollard finally sees his luck change after many years in the world of Depression-era horse racing, where jockeys were often treated with far less care than the horses they rode. In fact, Pollard has been on his own in that hardscrabble life since his parents abandoned him as a young teenager when the crash of 1929 left them unable to support him. He's generally considered too big to be a serious jockey, is blind in one eye after one too many bar fights for money, and is violently opposed to anything that looks like charity.

In other words, he's angry and bitter at the cards life has dealt him.

But now, being in the right place at the right time has put him in the saddle of an equally angry and troubled young racehorse named Seabiscuit. In many ways, they are a perfect match. All Pollard has to do is bring out the "diamond in the rough" that the horse's owner and trainer believe is in there. And to follow instructions. In one of the first big tests for Seabiscuit—a midlevel race in California—hopes are high for a win. Trainer Tom Smith lays out a strategy that involves hanging back for much of the race and carefully choosing the moment for speed.

However, soon after bolting from the starting gate, Pollard is cut off by another jockey. It reminds him of the kind of cutthroat racing he's grown up with. Incensed, he prods Seabiscuit to give chase, determined to get even. He abandons the race strategy and goes all out to act on his rage. Predictably, Seabiscuit loses the race by a wide margin. Commentators and spectators write off the horse and the jockey as too damaged to ever win anything.

When confronted by Smith after the race, Pollard rages, "He fouled me! What am I supposed to do? Let him get away with that?"

"Well, yeah, when he's forty to one!" Smith says.

The truth is, there is nothing wrong with Seabiscuit or with Red Pollard's skill as a jockey. Both have enormous potential to do great things, as the film goes on to prove. But in order to reach that potential, Red Pollard has to overcome a handicap every bit as real as his faulty eyesight: his inability to forgive and let go.

When Pollard fumed, "He fouled me!" he was not just talking about one jockey in one race. His response was fueled by everyone in a long list that included his own parents, who had made choices that caused him pain. His inability to forgive and move on was like an anchor dragging behind his life, making everything he did many times more difficult and prone to failure than it had to be. He, like so many people who suffer from depression today, could not conceive of letting go.

But it's not necessary to remain stuck there. You can break free. Much of our resistance to the idea of forgiveness begins with the fact that we don't truly understand what the word means.

Forgiveness: What It Isn't

To correct that, let's examine misconceptions about forgiveness that keep people stuck in bondage to their angry and fearful judgments.

Forgiveness isn't about letting someone "off the hook." The first and most powerful objection we encounter in ourselves is the mistaken idea that to forgive means looking the other way while somebody "gets away" with something. We see forgiveness as an undeserved get-out-of-jail-free card. That seems wrong somehow, because we can't stand the idea of saying "That's okay" about behavior that clearly is not.

The misunderstanding lies in the belief that forgiving someone is the same thing as excusing the offense. It isn't. In fact, the purpose of forgiveness is not to deliver anything at all to the one who caused us harm but to benefit *ourselves* by letting go of toxic attachment to the past and to our pain. So long as we hang on to feelings of outrage, injustice, and desire for payback, we keep the offense alive and the wounds fresh. And in the process, we remain vulnerable to all the negative physical and psychological effects of runaway anger and fear.

Think of it this way: somebody makes a choice that causes you harm and pain. That person is not a monster, just a flawed human being like everyone else. Once the offense has occurred, there is no longer anything you can do about it. The wrongdoing happened, period. But from that moment forward, what happens is *your* choice. Will you cling to the offense and its effects, keeping it alive and even making matters worse for yourself? Or will you let go of the need for "justice" and for answers to vague and useless questions like "Why me?"

If you take the first path, you'll trigger a chronic cascade of cortisol and adrenaline in your body, neurochemicals that have proven to adversely affect everything from brain function to blood pressure to immune system vitality, increasing the risk of all sorts of illness.

Essentially, you're choosing to respond to your pain by piling on even more. Not the wisest move. This is what is meant by the old proverb "Before you embark on a journey of revenge, dig two graves." It's impossible to hang on to judgment without harming yourself.

Forgiveness is the way out of this trap. Without making any excuses for the other person's bad behavior, and without shielding them from the consequences of their actions, you have the power to say, "I no longer hold this against you. I am moving on."

Forgiveness isn't a sign of weakness or an invitation to further offense. This fear appears to be rooted in the ancient human impulse to deal out judgment and retribution for personal or familial offenses. The belief was that if we don't take justice into our own hands, no one else will act on our behalf, leaving the door open for more trespasses of our boundaries.

And yet, ask yourself, Which is a bigger sign of weakness: letting the offensive actions of someone else determine your future health and well-being, or taking charge of your own destiny by choosing forgiveness over bondage to anger and fantasies of revenge? You could make a show of "strength" by stoking your anger and outrage indefinitely, but that's just illusion. You won't be weak by forgiving—just the opposite. As Chinese philosopher Lao Tzu wrote, "Mastering others is strength; mastering yourself is true power."

Forgiveness isn't the same thing as reconciliation. Most of the time, the goal after a painful conflict with someone we care about is to put the relationship back on track and move ahead with life. This is called reconciliation, a process that can serve to make us stronger and more tolerant of each other. In the case of most ordinary offenses, this is a good and healthy endeavor. Otherwise, we'd have no relationships at all, since it's impossible to go through life without occasionally stepping on each other's toes.

But while forgiveness is usually a necessary step in reconciliation, the inverse is not true. Sometimes a person's trespass is so harmful or severe that continuing the relationship is impossible or inadvisable. It's always possible to forgive in such cases, for reasons we've already discussed. But reconciliation is a different matter involving evidence of real remorse, restorative restitution, and future guarantees of safety. When healing from a serious offense, that's a high standard that requires the genuine participation of both parties for success.

As we employ forgiveness as a tool for healing depression, it's important that you don't confuse the two. If reconciliation is possible in your relationships that have been marred by offense and conflict, wonderful. You'll find that to be a source of healing as well. But if not, rest assured that forgiveness can still be your powerful ally.

Full-Spectrum Forgiveness

By looking closely at what forgiveness isn't, we've also begun forming a better idea of what it is—a get-out-of-jail-free card for *you*. That is, forgiveness is the way to liberate yourself from toxic attachments to old wounds and emotions that are directly responsible for your depression and other ill effects. Step one is accepting that this is true and that your freedom is worth the effort it will take to retrain yourself to let go. If you can get *there* and choose to honestly try forgiveness for a change, then the details of *how*—some of which you'll find in "Your Personal Action Plan" at the end of the chapter—will fall into place.

But first, we need to pick up one last bit of insight for the journey: a look at *all* those in need of your forgiveness. So far, we've talked only of people who have harmed or offended you in some way, and we've seen how an inability to forgive them keeps you enslaved to your pain. But those may not be the only ones against whom you harbor feelings of resentment and judgment.

Forgiving yourself. In many respects, this task is harder than grappling with the offenses of flesh-and-blood others. That's because things we hold against ourselves tend to be internal and unseen, which means "larger than life." As we lie awake in the wee hours of the morning, our own perceived offenses grow in our minds to monstrous proportions. They cease being about what we may have done and become damning evidence of who we are—*horrible human beings*. That, you may notice, is often the mind-set of people who suffer from depression, a deeply entrenched belief in their own worthlessness.

It's not true, of course. Take away the word *horrible*, and you've got the truth of it: we're all just human beings, flawed and prone to all kinds of blunders.

Have you made choices you are not proud of? Certainly.

Have you disappointed others who had a right to depend on you? Yes.

Have you betrayed someone's trust? Taken something that didn't belong to you? Lied to protect yourself from exposure? Exaggerated the truth just because you could? Cheated on an exam or another kind of test? Broken promises to God, yourself, or others? Put someone else in harm's way to gratify yourself?

Absolutely, and much more. How do I know? Because you are human, and every human on earth is a combination of strengths and weaknesses, assets and liabilities, successes and failures.

The irony is that we typically hold ourselves to a standard that's much higher than what we expect of others. It's an inverted kind of arrogance that causes us to set up a wall of shame in our minds, where all our flaws, large and small, are on display under bright light. When I was in the depths of my own depression, one of the most formidable obstacles I faced—one that almost scuttled my recovery before it could begin—was an inability to forgive myself for ever letting things get so bad. I saw failure and wreckage everywhere I looked and pointed a finger of blame directly at myself for all of it.

Here's the key to forgiveness when you're the one on trial: visualize yourself in court, but not as you appear today. See yourself as a child of six or seven. How would that child feel? Frightened? Alone? In need of comfort? Imagine taking a seat beside your small self and saying, "It's okay. You're learning. You'll be a better person because of this experience. Well done!" This is how to defeat the second of the three deadly emotions, guilt: by forgiving yourself.

Do that, and you'll be delighted to discover that the clouds of your depression begin to feel less dark and heavy.

Forgiving God. Whom do we blame for painful events that seem to come out of nowhere, beyond anyone's control? An improbable car crash that claims the life of someone we love? A tornado that destroys a hospital and kills innocent people? An illness that leaves us depleted and in pain? Business failure? Famine? War?

We blame God, of course—or "life"—for being cruel and unfair. Theologians and philosophers have wrestled for centuries with the question of why such things happen, and none has produced a universally satisfactory answer. We're simply left with a hard truth: bad things happen, and most of the time there's little or nothing to be done about it. Sometimes those events are unspeakably painful, and the temptation to give up on the very idea of a loving and omnipotent God is immense.

Yet clinging to universal resentment at "the way things are" is only a recipe for making your experience of them worse. Again, it is not necessary to say "It's okay" about something that clearly isn't. But it's also not okay to enslave yourself to misery by refusing to let go of your anger and pain. The key is in letting go of the need for explanations. Let God be God, and move on with your life. Chances are you'll never know why certain things happen . . . but you can know *peace* in spite of them.

Why Not?

Here's the bad news: if you choose not to forgive, you poison yourself, add more toxic shame to your life, and increase the desire to escape into unhealthy behaviors. And here's the good news: forgiveness is like a snowball rolling downhill. Once you get it moving, it keeps growing and picking up speed and growing some more. With the struggling clients I work with, I've seen time and time again that learning to forgive helps lighten their emotional load, brighten their outlook on life, shorten their recovery time, and restore their natural resilience against the recurrence of depression in the future.

While receiving assistance from professionals is usually helpful, the real key to your recovery is *you*. You are your own greatest ally and asset in your quest to heal your depression for life. That's because forgiveness will enable you to take a giant step toward wholeness, and forgiveness is something that can happen only within yourself. Far from being an abstract religious concept, deciding to follow God's urging to practice forgiveness is powerful progress in your journey back to wellness.

Why not believe it? Why not try?

Your Personal Action Plan

As I've pointed out, numerous studies have identified a strong link between forgiveness and depression recovery. That finding is intuitive once you consider the well-documented negative effects of clinging to resentment and anger. Even so, you might still be tempted to say, "That's all well and good for others, but I'm just not a very forgiving person."

There's good news for you, too. Those same studies have revealed that the ability to forgive can be *learned*. The power is yours, and you exercise it when you choose to try. Here's how to make forgiveness a part of your recovery:

1. **Make a clear choice.** If you've harbored resentment and a desire for revenge against someone for a long time, your

mind will resist your attempts to reverse direction and forgive. To signal that you are serious about getting free, create a contract with yourself. In your journal write, "I hereby pledge to forgive for the following offenses and for the following reasons." Be specific. Argue the case on paper for why forgiveness is the right choice at this time. Sign and date it, then put it somewhere you can easily reach when the going gets tough, as a "binding" reminder of your intention.

2. **Practice empathy.** As we've seen, it's important to think of those who have offended you as ordinary human beings, not monsters. Every human act—even a horrific one—springs from a person's own toxic mix of anger, guilt, fear, and woundedness. We all act as we do because on some level we feel that we must, given our life circumstances. While this is not a rationale for excusing others' bad behavior, it is an exercise in learning to walk in their shoes, see through their eyes, and hopefully find a reason for compassion. From there, it's much easier to contemplate forgiving them and moving on.

3. **Employ gratitude.** There are few things more powerful than listing all the things you are grateful for in your life. Write them down, say them out loud, and shout them if you can. Do this sincerely and consistently, and you'll soon realize your anger and pain at the unforgiven offense is not so hot or heavy as it was. That's because it's physically impossible to think two thoughts at once. You can't be grateful and harbor fantasies of revenge at the same time. When you choose to concentrate on the blessings you *do* have, what you've lost through someone else's behavior begins to look less scary and easier to simply let go of.

4. **Dwell in the present.** The truth is, any offense you have not yet forgiven exists only in the past—which is to say, only in your mind. The thief is not continuously breaking into your house; the assailant stopped harming you long ago, and your friend's betrayal happened only once. To stop reliving such events over and over, learn the art of mindfulness, of centering your thoughts in the safety of here and now. Many techniques exist for doing this. Find one that works for you and give it a try.

5. **Ask God for help.** Forgiveness does not come naturally to us in the wake of a painful trauma or offense. We must learn how to do it. We must learn how to truly *mean* it. Fortunately, the Great Teacher, our gracious heavenly Father, is ready to show us the way—when we ask.

CHAPTER 8

Strength through Soul Care

Spiritual Practices Are Essential to Healing from Depression

Way back in the introduction to this book, I shared with you my story of how I succumbed for a time to depression in my own life and nearly lost myself in the process. I told you how my family intervened and helped me set and enforce healthy boundaries for myself, involving many of the same treatments and choices you have now learned.

It's not unusual when I tell that story in group settings for someone to approach me afterward, still unsatisfied. They sense something is missing from my account because it sounds too simple, too formulaic.

"My family has tried everything yours did," one woman suffering from depression told me. "It's never enough. What made you so different?"

The only honest answer is *absolutely nothing*. I am no different, and certainly no better, than anyone else alive.

Yet the question brings up an important point. While there is nothing special about me, there was (and still is) something present in my life that played a powerful role in my recovery. It is an element that not everyone has yet discovered for themselves.

In a word: faith.

I grew up in Dodge City, Kansas, a place renowned for its farms, ranches, cowboys, and raucous Wild West history. Thankfully, I also grew up among devout Christian family members. Some of my earliest and fondest memories are set in church gatherings, surrounded by a community of people who had decided to give their lives to God. So when it was my turn later in life to stand on the edge of psychological and emotional oblivion in the form of depression, there was a dormant X factor buried in my heart and mind that, in the end, made all the difference. It's true that the loving intervention of my family and friends might not have been enough if I hadn't also had the learned instinct to cry out to someone much greater than myself with a single, simple plea: Help!

Soul Care Practices

Now, faith comes in many forms, and God can be found in many places. What follows is the road map and key landmarks I've drawn from my own Christian journey. My goal is not to impose my beliefs on you. Rather, these are practices drawn from my experience of faith that have proved to be effective spiritual tools for me and those we serve at The Center, and they will help you to care for your soul as you seek to heal depression for life.

Choose to Have Faith

In times of crisis, when well-meaning people advise you to "have faith," they often make it sound simple, as if it's possible to magically "have" something as elusive as faith on command. That's nearly as unhelpful as telling someone who's suffering from depression to simply "feel better." In previous chapters, you've learned that every step on the path to recovery requires courage and commitment on your part, all summed up in one powerful word: *choice*. You must choose to seek help and choose to pursue the remedies you are offered before you can tap into their healing potential.

Faith is no different. It's not an ethereal "thing" we try to grasp; it's more like an action—something we do on purpose. True, God is willing and able to meet you exactly where you are and to carry you for as long as it takes to restore your strength. In fact, I believe it would astonish us to see how often we benefit from God's unseen work around us. But faith is our part to play to actively complete the circuit of God's love. We do that by choosing to believe we are not alone—through sheer force of will, if necessary—when the night is at its darkest. God does not need our faith; we do. His strength does not wane; ours does.

Faith, precisely because it begins with a determined choice, is a jolt of energy that activates our spiritual and emotional immune system as nothing else can. How? By opening the door to the one thing that all people who suffer from depression feel they have lost forever: hope. As the writer of the book of Hebrews assures us, "Faith is confidence in what we hope for and assurance about what we do not see" (11:1).

That writer knew what it meant to hope for something we can't yet see, and he understood that active, determined faith sustains us while we wait for the thing we want to materialize and work to make it so. We might face a health crisis, relationship strain, job loss, or financial problems. Not every hardship we endure will turn out exactly the way we want, but we have the assurance that these things will ultimately result according to God's will and God's best for us. We have this confidence because our faith does not rest in fate or chance or any other thing on earth. Our faith is in God, who is unfailingly good.

One way or another, you always choose how to face your life, with confidence or with doubt, in strength or in defeat. Given those options, why not choose the power of faith?

Talk to God

Another way to care for your soul is to talk to God. You might be wondering, *Don't you mean "pray"?* That depends on your definition of that often misunderstood word. If by pray you mean "mutter a stream of rote, repetitive phrases you once heard in church"—things you'd never say to an intimate friend—then, no, that's definitely not what I mean. If prayer, to you, typically consists of a dreary session of complaining and self-condemning, that's also not what I have in mind.

Here's the point: the hope that's restored when you choose faith over despair is *real*. It's the priceless assurance that you are loved—beyond all reason—by a Creator who never takes his eyes off you for a second. He's the type who gleefully gets out his wallet to show off photos of all his children to anyone nearby.

What would you tell *that* person over a cup of tea today? Where it hurts? Your small (and large) victories? Your dreams and ambitions? Maybe your nightmares and disappointments? Would you ask some tough questions? Tell him what you fear? What you love? What you want? Would you laugh and cry together?

I believe you would. And you can. A heartfelt and honest conversation with God is yours for the having. Perhaps best of all, when talking with God, you can ask for wisdom and guidance amid all your struggles. Everyone on earth could use divine direction and understanding in their daily lives, and this is especially true for those battling depression. Prayer is a powerful source of insight and inspiration as you pursue healing.

Listen Closely

Many people scoff at the idea that God speaks back, but only because they've never heard an audible voice answer them directly. A key word when we think about prayer is *conversation*—two-way communication. Why bother to pray if we have no hope of receiving a reply? The truth is, God speaks all the time, and we would have no trouble hearing him if we'd only broaden our definition of speech. The psalmist wrote,

> The heavens declare the glory of God;
>   the skies proclaim the work of his hands.
> Day after day they pour forth speech;
>   night after night they reveal knowledge.
> They have no speech, they use no words;
>   no sound is heard from them.
> Yet their voice goes out into all the earth,
>   their words to the ends of the world.

PSALM 19:1-4

As this psalm so eloquently describes, God certainly speaks through nature. That message is one of majesty and grandeur, to be sure, but also of balance, beauty, and rebirth—qualities we can cling to in tough times.

That's just the beginning. Because God is the Creator, his voice can be heard all over his creation. God's voice can be heard in art and music and stories that inspire us to be more and do better. He speaks in every act of kindness, no matter how small. God's part of the conversation is found in sacred Scriptures and in the words of wise people throughout time who have labored to bring light into the darkness of ignorance. God speaks in our dreams and in subtle moments of intuition.

But as in every conversation, it's possible not to hear a word of it. Why? Because we're not listening. Until we choose to believe God will actually answer our questions and calm our fears, we may frantically do all the talking and never make room for his reply. To avoid this unnecessary mistake, we must slow down, set aside time to be quiet, and extend our awareness. If we go looking for the diverse love notes from God that litter the world, we will find them.

Cultivate Gratitude

Simply put, gratitude fosters optimism, which strengthens hope. That's why it's hard to imagine a more effective soul medicine than gratitude. Medieval Christian philosopher and mystic Meister Eckhart said, "If the only prayer you ever say in your entire life is thank you, it will be enough." The list of things we can and should be thankful for, even in our darkest moments, is practically inexhaustible.

Sometimes severe depression makes it hard to muster gratitude for the big things like being alive or the loved ones in your life. So start with the little ones. Anyone can come up with those—the more whimsical, the better.

For example, I'm grateful for ice cream and for the inspired genius who invented it. I'm glad that freshly mowed grass is part of my world on summer evenings, how it smells and how it feels on bare feet. How about you?

Try saying thank you—out loud and with gusto—for teriyaki sauce or butterflies or kites or Mozart . . . anything that has ever made you smile. Say thank you for hot showers and soft towels. Roller coasters. Baseball. Elvis Presley. Fireworks. Tulips poking out of the dirt. A child's unrestrained giggle. That magic moment when the lights go down in the movie theater.

I'm grateful for warm socks on a cold, rainy morning. And I'm not alone. Nobel Prize–winning Chilean poet Pablo Neruda wrote "Ode to My Socks," which concludes with these marvelous lines:

The moral
of my ode is this:
beauty is twice
beauty
and what is good is doubly
good

when it is a matter of two socks
made of wool
in winter.[1]

You get the idea. As the poet implies, gratitude is a multiplier, not of the beauty and good all around us in the world, but of our *awareness* of it. And gratitude also makes us more aware of the loving God responsible for it all. When dark thoughts threaten to push everything else aside, purposeful gratitude to our Creator is a powerful way to push back.

Come Clean about Your Mistakes

Even as a kid, I learned it was incredibly liberating to own up to something I'd done that I was not proud of. Trying to keep a dark secret from my parents, a teacher, or a friend was exhausting, like walking around with my pockets full of rocks. The moment I told the truth, it was as if the lights came on and all that weight disappeared. Even if there were still consequences to face, I learned that I always felt better to have the truth out in the open.

That is what the concept of confession is all about—setting us free from the dread of discovery when we're in the wrong. Like the active choice to have faith, this is not for God's benefit but for ours. Taking responsibility serves as a powerful reminder that we're only human after all. That is paradoxically empowering. Fear of exposure arises in part from the misguided belief that we ought to be more than we are, when the fact is God expects no such thing. The moment we admit our frailties, we find the strength and the motivation to be and do better in the future. Confession compels us to acknowledge who we are and to continually seek to improve.

What's more, confession puts us in the position to receive God's peace, comfort, and forgiveness. *Confess* has its origin in "agreement." So beyond the relief from worrying that we might be found out, confession means agreeing with God about our wrongdoing—and then agreeing with him in how we might work to make it right. The psalmist provides insight into the healing process: "When I kept silent, my bones wasted away through my groaning all day long. . . . Then I acknowledged my sin to you and did not cover up my iniquity. I said, 'I will confess my transgressions to the LORD.' And you forgave the guilt of my sin" (Psalm 32:3, 5).

Gather Together

One of the most formidable enemies facing people working to heal from depression is *isolation*. By ourselves, we're far more likely to get stuck in unhealthy habits and distorted thought patterns. Our lives become closed echo chambers endlessly reinforcing our sense of hopelessness and despair. What's needed to break through those lonely walls is a community of caring people willing to open their arms and make room for one more fellow traveler.

The right faith community can be just that. Most of my fellow Christians have come to their faith by one difficult road or another. People who share your faith will likely understand the challenges you face in your journey back from depression because they've walked a similar path. They'll provide a nonjudgmental shoulder to lean on.

Belonging to a faith community also provides a tangible reminder that you are not the only struggling person in the world. There's healing in remembering that life does not revolve around you and that even in your darkest moments, you are not uniquely alone. Furthermore, church gatherings will reveal that music, celebration, joy, gratitude, and service are all still alive and well in the world. A dozen or a hundred or a thousand voices all singing together can be a magical salve to a wounded heart.

Serve

Once you see you're not alone in your struggles, the next step is to reach outside of yourself to make a difference in someone else's life.

Faith communities usually excel at providing volunteer opportunities and steering you to the one that's right for you.

But even if involvement in a faith community is not your thing, you can find ample ways to be of use to your community if you look for them. Every major city in America has homeless shelters, counseling centers for victims of domestic violence, animal rescue organizations, wounded veterans programs, hospice centers, cancer support groups, suicide prevention clinics, nursing homes filled with people in need of a friend—the list could go on for pages. All of these programs depend on volunteers who know what it's like to need a boost. Best of all, the benefit of service is a two-way street, making life better for you as well as for those you help. A 2007 paper published by the Corporation for National and Community Service called *The Health Benefits of Volunteering* states, "Volunteer activities can strengthen the social ties that protect individuals from isolation during difficult times, while the experience of helping others leads to a sense of greater self-worth and trust."[2]

One study cited in the report concluded that people who volunteer in service to others live longer than those who don't.[3] Think of it this way: by getting involved in church outreach in your community, or by volunteering on your own, you essentially write yourself a prescription for relief from your troubles—free of charge!

Laugh

Sometimes wisdom can be found in unlikely places. That's certainly true of this lyric from a 1977 hit song by Jimmy Buffett: "If we couldn't laugh, we would all go insane."

I doubt the pop-music icon knew at the time that he had science on his side. The physical, psychological, and emotional payoff of laughter is no joke, as evidence is piling up that consistent laughter is good for you. Recent studies have detailed some of the benefits:

- reduced stress levels
- improved immune system function
- increased levels of endorphins, the body's natural painkillers
- increased heart rate and oxygenation of vital organs[4]

Beyond the scientifically proven benefits of laughter, can it really be considered a *spiritual* practice? Absolutely! Laughter is, in fact, a key advantage of the life of faith. God, our ultimate source of strength, gives us the gift of humor, levity, and wit as a way to savor life's good times and endure the bad times. The psalmist describes how God helped him to emerge from a season of sorrow and perhaps depression, and the result is laughter: "You have turned my mourning into joyful dancing. You have taken away my clothes of mourning and clothed me with joy, that I might sing praises to you and not be silent" (Psalm 30:11-12, NLT). In essence, accessing our God-given lightheartedness is a sure way to combat our downheartedness.

It might surprise you to learn that laughter, like the other practices in this chapter, is an activity you can choose to do, not simply something that happens spontaneously or not at all. "Laughter yoga," for example, is the practice of laughing on purpose in groups. It seems forced at first and downright silly. But the effort quickly turns into unprompted, genuine, impossible-to-resist laughter. Give yourself that experience, and you'll be astonished to realize the laughter was there inside you all along and will remain available anytime you need a boost.

Your Personal Action Plan

Soul care through faith is not simply a program to follow—it's a new way of life. It has the effect of transforming you from the inside out, shining a light on the old things that no longer serve you, and pointing to new ways of being that will. When faith works hand in hand with everything else you've learned in this book, the result can be breathtaking.*

Here are some first steps:

1. **Ask for divine help.** As Jesus told his followers, "Everyone who asks receives; the one who seeks finds; and to the one who knocks, the door will be opened" (Matthew 7:8). There is no more powerful prayer than a simple plea for help. Also, ask for God's wisdom as you seek to overcome depression and make decisions that will foster healing.

2. **Seek assistance and support from others.** If you've got persistent questions about the value and practice of faith, rest assured you're not the first one to ask them. Find someone you trust who can help you explore this topic. Others have walked the road ahead of you and can share what they've learned along the way.

3. **Read the Bible and other sacred texts.** The history of humanity is one long search for meaning and connection to our origins and true nature. Fortunately, there is a written record of the quest. Poets and mystics of all kinds have littered the road with breadcrumbs leading us back to ourselves—and to a loving, nurturing, healing God.

4. **Guard your thoughts.** Old ways of thinking and believing often put up a fierce fight when challenged by something new. You are not a mere bystander witnessing the battle, however. It's within your power to choose which thoughts and ideas you feed and which you starve. Each of us has a steady flow of

---

* If you're interested in learning more about the Christian use of these practices, as well as the scriptural basis for them, please see my book *Soul Care: Prayers, Scriptures, and Spiritual Practices for When You Need Hope the Most* (Carol Stream, IL: Tyndale, 2019).

words and messages continually filling our minds. This self-talk can be a strong influence on our feelings, choices, and perspectives—positive or negative. Nurture the helpful, healing thoughts while banishing the ones that bring you down and cause you to doubt.

5. **Regularly pause to say thank you.** As I said earlier, gratitude is a key component in the healing of depression. Yet many people overlook the blessings in their lives or can't embrace the good when they feel so bad. Make a choice each day to be grateful. Keep a gratitude journal. Before sleep, review the gifts that came your way. On a walk with a friend, mention some things you're grateful for. Pray with a particular focus on thankfulness.

PART 3

Body

CHAPTER 9

Start Moving and Start Improving

Physical Activity Provides a Massive Boost to Your Mood and Metabolism

If Gina didn't set an alarm for 2:40 in the afternoon, the chances were very good that she would forget to pick up her daughter from kindergarten.

Gina was deeply depressed, and her emotions and behaviors showed it. She felt sad and numb. She had little energy for the tasks of daily life. Most days, she woke up long enough to drive her daughter, Lexie, to school; then she came home and slept or stared out the picture window in the living room until it was time to pick Lexie up. As soon as dinner was over, Gina would crawl back under the covers, leaving her husband, Steve, to finish out the evening with their five-year-old.

One day Steve begged Gina to take an online depression screening, and neither was surprised when her scores indicated she was clinically depressed.

The couple came to The Center: A Place of Hope convinced that

Gina needed to start on antidepressants. After visiting with the two of them and reviewing medical history and lab work, Gina's physician said, "You could go on antidepressants, but I believe walking for thirty minutes five times a week will do as much good or more as medication."

A lot was going on in Gina's life, body, and brain that had been contributing to her depression, and the whole-person plan we designed for her tackled the problem from many angles. But a critical part of that plan was getting Gina moving again.

The idea that exercise can alleviate and even prevent depression is not a new one. Neither is the idea that, in some cases, exercise can be as effective as antidepressants in stabilizing or improving moods.

In one study, 156 adults with major depressive disorder were randomized into three groups. The first group participated in aerobic exercise sessions three times a week; the second group was given an antidepressant; and the third group participated in a combination of exercise and medication.

After four months, the group that participated in exercise alone benefited *as much as the other two groups.* It's especially interesting that participants in the exercise-only group were also less likely to relapse into depression, and those who exercised regularly during a ten-month follow-up period were less likely (by more than 50 percent) than non-exercisers to be depressed.[1]

The study is one of many with similar findings. In fact, professors from the University of Toronto analyzed twenty-six years of research on the link between depression and exercise. Their conclusion, based on their review of more than twenty-five different research articles, was that even low levels of physical activity for twenty to thirty minutes a day could reduce or prevent depression in people of all ages.

"This review shows promising evidence that the impact of being active goes far beyond the physical," explained George Mammen, coauthor of the review. "If you're currently active, you should sustain it. If you're not physically active, you should initiate the habit."[2]

Start Somewhere

I have to admit that when I'm talking with our clients, I often substitute a different term for the word *exercise*. Some people associate the word with such grueling discomfort or past monumental efforts and failures that they immediately put up resistance to the idea.

Instead, I use the phrase "physical movement."

Instead of telling depressed clients to begin an exercise program, I talk to them about moving more and increasing their activity. Many depressed individuals have such low energy and low motivation that exercise is the last thing they want to do. One of my clients found exercising such a daunting challenge that she discovered a *very* gradual way to get started. She simply made it her daily goal to get dressed in her gym clothes, drive to the gym, and stand on the treadmill. That was all.

Well, it was a start. If she did those three things, she considered her goals met for the day. This effectively eliminated the "I'm too tired" excuse. Whenever she had that thought, she reminded herself that she didn't have to actually *do* anything; she just had to stand on the treadmill, which of course took little effort.

Her strategy also took care of the "I don't have time to work out" excuse. Whenever she had that thought, she reminded herself she didn't have to spend much time at the gym—she just had to stand for a moment on the treadmill, which of course took little time at all.

You can imagine what happened next. More often than not, by the time this woman drove to the gym and stood on the treadmill, her next thought was, *As long as I'm here, I might as well walk for ten minutes.* In the weeks ahead, ten minutes became twenty, then forty, and by the end of the year she had lost twenty pounds, had improved her eating habits, and was sleeping better at night. Her energy level had rebounded, along with her self-esteem. Her symptoms of depression did not magically vanish altogether, but she felt the renewed vitality and optimism to begin addressing other aspects of her life that would lead her toward healing.

This woman was wise in discerning that she needed to train her schedule and her willpower before she began training her body. And it worked. By starting slow, we give our bodies, routines, and self-discipline time to catch up to what our brains know we need to do. The important thing is to begin doing *something*, no matter how small or simple.

The Magic Hour

To combat depression, you don't need to hire a personal trainer or spend hours at the gym (although I would encourage both options). You can improve your mobility and mental health by consistently choosing to move more in simple ways. For example, try parking a little farther from your workplace, taking the stairs instead of the elevator, walking the dog after dinner, spending thirty minutes a day gardening, or meeting a friend several times a week for a stroll through a park.

A study published in the *American Journal of Psychiatry* followed 33,908 healthy adults for eleven years and tracked data related to exercise, depression, and anxiety. The researchers concluded that sedentary participants were 44 percent more likely to develop depression than participants who exercised just one to two hours a week. In fact, that one-hour mark was particularly significant. Here are some of the conclusions of the study:

- When it came to protecting people from depression, most of the benefits were realized with an hour of low-level exercise a week.

- Low-intensity exercises were just as beneficial as high-intensity exercises.
- Future cases of depression could have been prevented among 12 percent of the study's participants if they had engaged in at least one hour of physical activity each week.[3]

The benefits of even moderate physical activity are widespread and substantial. According to Dr. Alpa Patel, strategic director of the American Cancer Society's Cancer Prevention Study-3, "When you go from doing no activity to any amount, you see a marked decline in the risk of premature death from any cause."[4] I am struck by that amazing sequence of words: *any amount . . . marked decline . . . from any cause.*

Of course, there are additional benefits from consistent workouts of higher intensity. According to the Physical Activity Guidelines for Americans, your weekly activity goal should include two and a half hours of moderate-intensity aerobic activity (such as brisk walking) and two days of muscle-strengthening activities that work all major muscle groups (legs, hips, back, abs, chest, shoulders, and arms). Meeting these guidelines can literally save your life, creating dramatic improvements related to diabetes, heart health, bone and muscle strength, and more.[5]

But studies show that when it comes to mental health, increasing your activity level even a small amount—especially if you've been sedentary—matters. A lot.

How Physical Movement Helps Depression

Why is moving so important? John Ratey, MD, author of the book *Spark: The Revolutionary New Science of Exercise and the Brain,* calls depression a "physical alteration of the brain's emotional circuitry." Here's how he explains what is happening in the depressed brain:

Norepinephrine, dopamine, and serotonin are essential messengers that ferry information across the synapses, but without enough good connections in place, these neurotransmitters can only do so much. As far as the brain is concerned, its job is to transfer information and constantly rewire itself to help us adapt and survive. In depression, it seems that in certain areas, the brain's ability to adapt grinds to a halt. The shutdown in depression is a shutdown of learning at the cellular level. Not only is the brain locked into a negative loop of self-hate, but it also loses the flexibility to work its way out of the hole.

He adds, "If your prefrontal cortex has been offline for a while, you need to reprogram it, and exercise is the perfect tool."[6]

When it comes to reprogramming the depressed brain, why is exercise so invaluable? When you exercise, your body increases the release of critical chemicals and hormones that have a major impact on brain health and mood. Here are five brain chemicals and hormones that are impacted by exercise.

Norepinephrine

Both a hormone and a brain chemical, norepinephrine makes you more alert while improving focus, memory, and concentration. This is why exercise was proven to improve cognitive control in children with ADHD in a study conducted at the University of Illinois. In this study, children who participated in just twenty minutes of exercise performed better on tests and had an easier time focusing.[7]

Dopamine

This is a neurotransmitter linked to pleasure and motivation. It also helps you plan ahead, concentrate, and experience feelings of joy and accomplishment when you reach your goal. Physical movement is one of the most effective natural methods of increasing dopamine. What's more, if your activity takes place outside, you're even better off, since sunlight also helps by increasing the number of dopamine receptors and creating vitamin D, which aids in the release of dopamine.

Serotonin

This brain chemical is a natural mood stabilizer that significantly impacts your emotions, but it also helps regulate appetite, sleep, memory, sexual desire, and social behavior. Exercise not only increases serotonin production, but it also improves how your body utilizes it.

Brain-Derived Neurotrophic Factor (BDNF)

This chemical promotes the growth of new connections between brain cells, making it extremely crucial to overall brain health. Exercise can triple the production of BDNF in your brain.

Endorphins

These neurochemicals minimize discomfort and stress. They are, in fact, your brain's natural painkillers and are linked to feelings of euphoria and general well-being. University of Turku researchers identified a particular kind of exercise—high-intensity interval training—that created the biggest boost in endorphin release.

Dr. Ratey concludes, "Exercise is not an instant cure, but you need to get your brain working again, and if you move your body your brain won't have any choice. It's a process, and the best strategy is to take it one step—and then one stride—at a time. Start slowly and build on it. At its core, depression is defined by an absence of moving toward anything, and exercise is the way to divert those negative signals and trick the brain into coming out of hibernation."[8]

But Wait, There's More

Clients of mine who start moving—and then stay moving as a cornerstone of a healthier lifestyle—are more successful at reducing or eliminating symptoms of depression, now and in the future. And yet the benefits of moving more don't stop there.

"Exercise is the magic pill," says Dr. Michael Bracko, chairman of the American College of Sports Medicine's Consumer Information Committee, adding that "exercise can literally cure diseases like some forms of heart disease. Exercise has been implicated in helping people prevent or recover from some forms of cancer. Exercise helps people with arthritis. Exercise helps people prevent and reverse depression."[9]

You already know that exercise is good for your whole body. But let me highlight some of the most important health benefits here. Physical movement helps to . . .

- **Strengthen bones.** Weight-bearing exercises strengthen muscles by causing new bone tissue to grow. When you think of weight-bearing exercises, you may think immediately of lifting weights, but "weight-bearing exercises" also refers to movements that cause you to support the weight of your own body. These include walking, jogging, climbing stairs, dancing, and even jumping. Non-weight-bearing exercises include swimming and bicycling.
- **Build muscles.** Muscle-building exercises are increasingly important as we age, as the human body begins losing muscle mass from about the age of thirty. When we refuse to let nature take its course and become intentional about moving in ways that help us maintain and even build muscle, we reap the benefits in nearly every area of life. Besides the obvious perks (like having an easier time picking up kids and grandkids or carrying groceries in from the car), stronger

muscles improve balance and reduce the likelihood of falls as we age. Plus, stronger muscles help maintain bone mass, reducing our chances of developing osteoporosis.

- **Provide a better night's sleep.** We've already examined the link between depression and sleep and shown how consistently getting a solid night's sleep can dramatically improve emotional health. According to one study, people with chronic insomnia who engaged in medium-intensity aerobic exercise (such as walking) fell asleep quicker and slept longer.[10]

- **Support cardiovascular health.** Every year, about 735,000 American adults have a heart attack. In fact, heart disease is the leading cause of death for men and women, killing more than 600,000 people in the United States every year.[11] Study after study shows that physical inactivity is a significant risk factor for heart disease and that exercise can dramatically reduce your risk of developing heart disease—and can even help reverse damage that has already occurred. But collectively, we're still not moving nearly enough. Four out of five adults don't meet the Physical Activity Guidelines for heart health recommended by the US Department of Health and Human Services. Four of the best exercises for a healthy heart are brisk walking, running, swimming, and bicycling.

- **Lower blood sugar.** Exercise lowers blood sugar by increasing insulin sensitivity. This helps your muscle cells use available insulin to take up glucose during and after your workout. The contraction of your muscles during exercise also improves the way your cells absorb and use glucose, even without insulin.[12]

Alter Your Attitude

In addition to doing wonders for your brain and body, physical movement can be a game changer when it comes to your overall attitude and mind-set. Dr. Ratey talks about exercise being the perfect tool for reprogramming a depressed prefrontal cortex. It can reprogram how you think and cope too. Here's what else regular movement is going to do for you:

- **Increase your confidence.** There's the confidence that comes from having a body that is fit and healthy, and there is also confidence that comes from doing something every day that you know is good for you. Either way, regular physical movement empowers you to feel better about yourself.
- **Boost your creativity.** Research conducted at Stanford University showed that something as simple as casual walking improves creativity by boosting convergent thinking (solving a problem) as well as divergent thinking (coming up with original ideas).[13]
- **Help you cope.** We've already talked about the fact that the endorphins released while exercising serve as your body's natural painkillers while helping to reduce anxiety and stress. That makes exercise the perfect go-to activity when you're looking for a healthy coping strategy. Unhealthy coping techniques (such as misusing alcohol, overeating, and excessive TV viewing) may provide a temporary release or escape, but they are expedient at best and cause more harm than good in the end. Physical movement, however, is a coping strategy that not only provides relief in the moment, but it also offers innumerable lasting benefits for a healthy brain and body.

Ready, Set, Go!

When I told Gina to begin her journey to wellness by placing one foot in front of the other, she resisted. Tearing up, she told me she had neither the energy nor the desire to move more than she already did . . . which amounted to getting herself to the car and back a couple of times a day.

But a few weeks later, when a neighbor suggested a short walk every morning after Gina returned from taking Lexie to school, Gina agreed to get outside her comfort zone and muster the energy to start slowly.

The first three mornings, the two women walked just a few blocks. Gina had been afraid that her neighbor would be frustrated by the slow pace and short distance. But she soon discovered that her neighbor had her own struggles she was dealing with and was filled with nothing but compassion and understanding for Gina.

Gina opted for consistency over intensity. She focused more on getting out her front door every morning rather than pushing herself to walk farther than she felt comfortable. Within a week, the two women were walking twice as far—plus, Gina realized their growing companionship and daily conversation provided much-needed support as she began to slowly navigate her way out of the darkness and into the light. In the months ahead, this consistent physical movement, and the camaraderie that came with it, became a cornerstone of Gina's healing.

Exercise is such a powerful resource because the impact is so comprehensive. In fact, time after time, I see the power of movement become a catalyst for transformation in many areas in my clients' lives.

So, when you're finished with this chapter, take a break from your reading and go for a walk or a bike ride. Start moving, and soon you'll find your emotional health improving.

Your Personal Action Plan

Increasing your activity level for one day is a great start, but the most powerful benefits will come from consistency. Once you get moving, how do you keep moving, day after day, week after week? Here are five ways to reap the long-term benefits of a more active lifestyle:

1. **Keep a journal.** Write down what your thoughts and feelings were like before, during, and after exercising. Write about any improvements you feel in your body, attitude, or emotions. You can also journal about any new thoughts you had during or after exercising—after all, we know that exercise is linked with creativity and problem solving, so you never know what hopeful, helpful ideas you might discover.

2. **Be consistent.** Especially as you get started, remember that consistency is more important than intensity. As you gain strength in your body and mind, you may naturally want to increase the intensity of your workouts. In the beginning, however, make consistency your number one goal, and the rest will follow.

3. **Ban all-or-nothing thoughts.** Consistency and commitment are indeed essential for an effective activity regimen, but don't be hard on yourself if you slack off a bit. Perfectionism is the enemy of progress . . . and all-or-nothing thinking has ended many exercise programs before they really got going. If you miss a day, or a few, don't think too much about it. Just start moving again. Just as consistency is more important than intensity, it's also more important than maintaining a perfect record. Don't let setbacks derail your strategic, health-enhancing goals.

4. **Enlist the help of fitness apps.** Downloading a fitness app on your phone or purchasing an activity tracker isn't necessary (so don't put off your fitness goals until you have one) but can be motivating for some people. If counting steps or reaching activity goals by using an app or tracker feels rewarding, do it!

5. **Create a favorite workout playlist.** Music and movement are a powerful combination. Creating a playlist of lively tunes that make you want to move is always a great idea, plus the association day after day will become a familiar cue to which your brain and body will respond.

CHAPTER 10

Good Food = Good Mood

Proper Nutrition and Hydration Fortify Your Body to Fend Off Depression

Every gardener knows that plants can't grow without the essential elements of water, light, and properly balanced soil. If you have too much water, you will drown your plants. Too little, and they will starve. Too little light, and they will wither. Too much, and they will burn. As for the soil, only the appropriate balance of nutrients and minerals will allow your garden to thrive.

Our bodies respond in the same way. Without the proper balance of the right elements, our bodies will not thrive. And when I say "our bodies," this of course means *everything* about our physical makeup: our brain function, metabolism, muscle tone, bone strength, energy level, immune system efficiency, sexual vitality, digestive health, and on and on. And when I say "the right elements," this means proper nutrition and hydration—food and drink that empowers the body to function at its optimal capacity. The right food will provide the right results.

We sometimes hear it said of Olympic athletes or others who physically perform at a high level, "Her body is a well-oiled machine!" I have news for you: God created *your* body to be a well-oiled machine, too, whether or not you run marathons, swim a hundred laps every day, or cycle long distances. The psalmist had a more poetic description of the human body, saying we are "fearfully and wonderfully made" by our Creator (Psalm 139:14). Your body and mind form an intricate, delicate system . . . and this system is fueled and fortified by nutrient-rich foods also wonderfully made by our Creator. God designed our bodies and the earth's rich food sources to work in harmony, bringing us maximum health and wellness.

Here's the key point for this chapter: nutritious, fortifying foods support not only physical health but mental health as well. Over the past few decades, numerous research studies have demonstrated again and again the undeniable link between proper nutrition and mental health. I appreciate the words of Harvard Medical School's Monique Tello, MD, who says, "Diet is such an important component of mental health that it has inspired an entire field of medicine called nutritional psychiatry. . . . What it boils down to is that what we eat matters for every aspect of our health, but especially our mental health. Several recent research analyses looking at multiple studies support that there is a link between what one eats and our risk of depression, specifically."[1]

Though I will provide lots of practical information in the pages ahead, the essential message of this chapter is simple and straightforward: what you put in your mouth each day affects your mood and mental health directly and dramatically.

Be Careful What You Consume

When it comes to nutritional imbalance or deficiency, a high-sugar, high-fat diet is the most pervasive culprit. Evidence of this is easy to see if you consider all the medical literature focused on the addictive-ness of sugar and fats.

The insidious part of this particular problem is that sugar isn't *just* sugar. Modern food and drink manufacturers sneak sugar into nearly all processed foods as a flavor enhancer. Many foods, even foods you might not consider "sweet," have added sugar, often in the form of high-fructose corn syrup. Apple juice and cranberry juice blends, for example, beyond their natural sweetness, often have a lot of added fructose in them.

I'd wager the average American is so used to sweetened foods that it's a main reason why genuinely healthy foods don't "taste good" to so many people struggling to change their eating habits. To make matters worse, most people who aren't on a low-carb diet tend to forget the sugar content in many alcoholic drinks, as well as the negative effect that alcohol in general can have on the body's blood sugar levels. And regular, responsible alcohol consumption is a fairly normal part of many cultures' diets.

Using artificial sweeteners doesn't let you off the hook either, and just avoiding sugar isn't enough. That's because even a diet that is fairly balanced in terms of carbohydrates but is high in fats (even so-called "good" fats) will throw your system out of whack. As anyone who has dieted can tell you, the issue isn't as simple as just changing what you eat and drink. Habits can be very difficult to break, and some research shows there are physiological issues that pose a challenge too.

A study conducted at the University of Georgia at Athens fed a population of rats two different diets: one well balanced with proteins, fats, and carbohydrates; the other with a significantly higher fat content. Over the course of two months, the rats that ate the higher-fat diet not only ended up significantly larger than their healthier counterparts, but the balance of their gut bacteria had also been altered.

According to Dr. Krzysztof Czaja, the neuroscientist who presented the findings, this bacterial imbalance actually damaged the vagus nerve (which connects the brain to the gut) such that it no longer properly transmitted satiety signals to the brain.[2] In other words, this destructive diet caused lasting damage that might make it difficult for the rats ever to feel full—whether or not they ever shifted to a healthier menu.

As with so many things in the body, the effect of any one possible contributor to depression is not isolated. For instance, we know that antibiotics can disrupt proper digestion and absorption of nutrients, and we know the strong influence of dietary choices. But new studies show that the combination of these factors can lead to substantially greater problems than either one alone. In another study, mice were given penicillin *and* fed a high-fat diet. These rodents developed more body fat and had higher insulin levels (which leads to the development of type 2 diabetes) than mice exposed to either antibiotics or the high-fat diet alone and compared to mice exposed to neither microbiotic offender.

Further, a group of studies demonstrated that aspartame—the key sweetener in many diet drinks and other artificially sweetened, low-calorie foods—caused an even higher level of insulin resistance, consistent with the elevated risk of diabetes. The researchers reported that the aspartame had supported the overgrowth of bacteria strains known to affect insulin tolerance negatively. In short, using aspartame ultimately causes us to crave yet more sweetness, which dumps us in a destructive cycle.

These are but a few examples to illustrate a point: we need to be extremely careful about what we consume, because many studies are proving that the typical diet these days contains substances that greatly affect our physical and mental health. Many of these substances we simply take for granted or ignore as part of "normal" food production and preparation.

With a delicate ecosystem like the human body, introducing harmful elements creates a ripple effect throughout the entire system.

As a result, to resolve any contributors to depression in this area, we must seek to restore and maintain balance with foods that offer robust vitamins and minerals. For everyone seeking optimal health—and especially those struggling to overcome depression—we should be on red alert about the many ways our modern culture is undermining our efforts to achieve wellness . . . and much of this pertains to the food and drink choices we are presented with every day.

Foods That Contribute to Depression

Obviously, there are scores of helpful books available that dive deeply into the benefits and tools of good nutrition (some are listed in appendix 4, "Recommended Resources," in the back of this book). Within the context of our discussion here, I want to highlight some basic yet essential guidelines related to what you eat and drink and how your body can thrive, even when you are depressed.

Even more relevant to the goal of this book, we will focus on what foods actually *contribute to* depression and what foods help *combat* its debilitating effects. That is the good news: there are foods and liquids that have been scientifically proven to help fend off depression.

Let's start with what we *don't* want to put in our bodies. Below are some of the main culprits leading to nutritional imbalance. A phrase I often use to point out the five main mischief-makers in our culture's diet is "devitalized food." By this, I am talking about food that has had virtually every good or "vital" thing stripped or removed from it. The "Big 5" include:

1. Processed foods
2. Junk foods
3. White flour
4. White rice
5. Refined sugar

You'll notice that most of the elements I mention above are white in color—white rice, white flour, white sugar: all processed, and all bad for you. And devitalized foods are the ones that are the most tempting: the quick burger and fries at the drive-thru as you rush home exhausted after a long day. Or those processed cookies on the grocery store shelf that taste so good as you relax in front of the TV at night.

They are hard to resist. But if we are serious about conquering depression, we need to wage war on the worst dietary offenders. Yes, it may mean cooking after a long day when you don't feel like it. Or it may mean eating foods that don't have the same sweet-and-savory "zing" as those deep-fried foods that deliver empty calories and bad ingredients.

Here's the insidious fact: when your energy levels are down from depression, these quick foods can be highly tempting and temporarily satisfying. Gulp down that sugary caffeine drink and—*bam!*— instant energy. You'll feel the jolt, all right . . . until you crash an hour later and feel even worse than you did before. That is not a good strategy for combating depression.

The devitalized foods and drinks I refer to provide only *fragmented* nutrition, meaning they contain only a small amount of what your body needs. Right alongside fragmented foods (such as the "white foods" mentioned above) are their equally destructive cousins, the junk foods. Common ingredients in junk foods include additives, preservatives, pumped-up or masked sugars (sucrose, fructose, and so on), fats, salts, artificial colors, and food dyes.

Like many things when it comes to human biology and physiology, everyone is different. While some people can drink a cup of coffee at 11:00 p.m. and fall right to sleep, others stay awake all night if they've had caffeine eight hours before bedtime. But there are general rules to follow and foods and beverages to avoid if you are struggling with depression. Here are the main types:

1. **Caffeine.** Not only can caffeine be addictive, but once the thrill is gone, it might even exacerbate your depression by making you more anxious and nervous.

2. **Alcohol.** This is a depressant, which means it reduces your brain's serotonin, a neurotransmitter that acts as a mood stabilizer. Alcohol can also act as a stimulant and increase anxiety and stress.

3. **Additives.** I want to highlight two particularly unhealthy additives that you will find in a surprising amount of foods and beverages: monosodium glutamate (MSG) and aspartame. As touched on before, studies have shown that aspartame—a common artificial sweetener—can cause DNA damage, increase obesity, and contribute to depression symptoms. MSG, like aspartame, may also interfere with the balance of neurotransmitters in your brain, leading to depression.

4. **Processed foods.** Stay away from processed foods as much as possible, including hot dogs, most deli meats (unless organic and fresh), and fried foods. Another subtle culprit: margarine. Stick to real butter, as margarine is high in unhealthy transfatty acids, along with coloring additives and emulsifiers.

5. **Refined sugars.** Avoid foods high in refined sugar, like cookies, most juices, and of course candy. The trouble is they have a detrimental effect on your blood sugar levels as they contain no fiber. This means that when your system is flush with refined sugar, it causes your glucose levels to fluctuate dramatically, which in turn can lead to anxiousness, irritability, and depression.

6. **Nonorganic or "conventional" foods.** Sometimes it's hard to get to the organic source of things, especially when it comes

to eating. But the more organic (i.e., natural, from-the-source, unprocessed) food you can eat, the more you are making food your ally rather than your enemy in your fight against depression.

Foods That Help Relieve Depression

It would be nice if medical science identified a quick-fix "magic formula" for combating depression through nutrition. Imagine if your physician or nutritionist handed you a prescription and said, "Eat five kumquats, twenty broccoli florets, and a handful of pine nuts twice a day—and your depression will lift in a month."

Nutritional eating isn't quite that simple . . . but neither is it overly complex. The matter often comes down to common sense. You know a party-size bag of potato chips and a liter of cherry soda will taste great while you watch the football game on Sunday afternoon. But you also know this taste-bud-tantalizing snack will deliver only empty calories, providing virtually no fortifying nutrition but infusing you with plenty of additives and artificial coloring agents. You also know you'll score points with your coworkers when you bring a big box of donuts into the office break room . . . at least until midmorning, when there is a collective sugar-high crash and productivity plummets. Your coworkers might also feel irritated toward you when they step on the scale at the gym after work.

Maybe you should listen to the wise words your mother used to tell you when you were growing up: "Eat your fruits and vegetables . . . and stay away from cake and candy." Parents' advice isn't always on target, but in this case it certainly is. By steering you toward plants and away from sweets, Mom was definitely pointing you in the right direction.

In case you need more scientific substantiation, understand that researchers have come a long way in identifying the best and worst foods to consume for mental health. In the latest meta-analysis examining the associations between dietary habits and depression risks, researchers reported,

> A dietary pattern characterized by a high intake of fruit,
> vegetables, whole grain, fish, olive oil, low-fat dairy
> and antioxidants and low intakes of animal foods was
> apparently associated with a decreased risk of depression.
> A dietary pattern characterized by a high consumption of
> red and/or processed meat, refined grains, sweets, high-fat
> dairy products, butter, potatoes and high-fat gravy, and
> low intakes of fruits and vegetables is associated with an
> increased risk of depression.[3]

Let's break this down into more specifics about a nutrition-rich diet that will help relieve your depression. Everyone likes the idea of "eating healthy," but what does that look like day in and day out? Here are several helpful strategies—along with specific food recommendations—that will enrich your body and lift your mood.[4]

Avoid cell damage with antioxidants. You've probably heard the term "free radicals" and might have thought they were involved in some kind of protest movement left over from the sixties. Well, they are a kind of protest movement, only taking place in your body. Essentially, free radicals are atoms that are unstable. They can harm your body's cells, resulting in illness and signs of aging, among other things.

Our bodies normally make these molecules, which put our bodies—and especially our brains—at risk. It's impossible to fully thwart free radicals, but by consuming antioxidant-heavy foods, you can reduce their impact on your body. These include:

- beta-carotene: apricots, broccoli, cantaloupes, carrots, collards, peaches, pumpkin, spinach, sweet potatoes

- vitamin C: blueberries, broccoli, grapefruits, kiwis, oranges, peppers, potatoes, strawberries, tomatoes
- vitamin E: wheat germ, nuts and seeds, vegetable oils

Be "carb conscious." Serotonin, the mood-altering brain chemical, has been shown to be affected by carbohydrates. Researchers speculate that an individual's craving for carbs is related to low serotonin activity. What's more, some carbs have been shown to have a calming effect, while others do not. It's best to avoid sugary foods and to consume "smart" or "complex" carbs (such as whole grains) rather than simple carbs, often found in baked goods.

Provide your brain with healthy proteins. The amino acid tryptophan (found in turkey, tuna, chicken, and similar foods) boosts your brain's production of serotonin. So try to eat protein-rich foods several times a day, especially when your energy level needs a lift. Healthy choices include beans and peas, lean beef, low-fat cheese, fish, milk, poultry, soy products, and yogurt. As I've said elsewhere, avoid processed proteins—such as packaged lunch meats and wrapped cheese slices—and look for organic choices instead.

Be "vitamin B aware." Several research studies have demonstrated the link between vitamin B_{12} deficiency and depression. For instance, one study of more than four thousand men and five thousand women found that rates of depression tended to rise in men—especially smokers—who were deficient in folate. The same thing happened for women—especially for those who smoked or didn't exercise—when they lacked vitamin B_{12}. B vitamins and folate can be found in legumes, nuts, many fruits, dark green vegetables, and low-fat animal products, such as fish and low-fat dairy products.

Make vitamin D a must-have. In a 2013 meta-analysis, researchers concluded that a deficiency in vitamin D results in a higher risk of suffering from depression. Because vitamin D is essential to the brain, low levels of it can be a factor in depression and other mental illnesses.

In another study, University of Toronto researchers noticed that people who had symptoms of depression, particularly seasonal affective disorder, tended to improve when the amount of vitamin D in their bodies increased as it typically does during the spring and summer.

To ensure you're getting enough vitamin D, consume plenty of salmon, egg yolks, yogurt, whole milk, almond milk, orange juice, oatmeal, cheese, shiitake mushrooms, and fortified tofu.

Don't skimp on selenium. Studies have shown a connection between low selenium and depression. For adults, the recommended amount for selenium is 55 micrograms per day. I believe that nutritional supplements can help counterbalance a deficiency, but it's always best to fortify your body with healthy foods, such as these:

- beans and legumes
- lean meat (lean pork and beef, skinless chicken and turkey)
- low-fat dairy products
- nuts and seeds (particularly brazil nuts—but no more than one or two a day because of their high selenium content)
- seafood (oysters, clams, sardines, crab, saltwater fish, and freshwater fish)
- whole grains (whole-grain pasta, brown rice, oatmeal, etc.)

Optimize your diet with omega-3 fatty acids. According to researchers, major depressive disorders occur at higher rates among those who are lacking in omega-3s, and depression is more likely to occur in people who seldom eat fish (a common source of omega-3s). Good sources of omega-3s include:

- fatty fish (anchovies, mackerel, salmon, sardines, shad, and tuna)
- flaxseed
- canola and soybean oils

- nuts, especially walnuts
- dark green, leafy vegetables

Find more fiber. Replace foods high in sugar and fat with those high in fiber. This includes vegetables such as asparagus, Jerusalem artichokes, broccoli, Brussels sprouts, cabbage, cauliflower, collard greens, kale, leeks, and onions, as well as bananas, legumes, and nuts. This also includes whole grains, such as barley, whole wheat, and oats. Fiber plays an important role in regulating your digestive system and helping you feel fuller so you have fewer cravings.

Chocolate lovers, rejoice—indulge and feel good. You may be pleased to know that eating chocolate really can make you happier! Studies have shown that dark chocolate increases the growth of two bacteria strains in particular that are top producers of gamma-aminobutyric acid (GABA) in the body. GABA is a neurotransmitter, like serotonin, that helps regulate your body's anxiety level and mood.

Chocolate has components that act as a prebiotic, making your gut environment more fertile ground for these two GABA-secreting strains. If you opt for dark chocolate with 75 percent cacao or more, you'll naturally be led toward low-sugar treats.

Replace Unhealthy with Healthy Choices

It's fine to know what's *not* helpful to consume and what is helpful . . . but how about some ideas for what to replace some of that bad stuff with? Here they are:

Instead of caffeine-based coffee and black tea, *swap with* herbal and green teas with less or no caffeine, or decaf coffee, black. Also try chamomile, lemon balm, peppermint, rosemary, and turmeric tea, the latter of which has been used for centuries in Chinese medicine as a treatment for depression.

Instead of a steady intake of alcoholic drinks high in sugars, such as spirits, *swap with* red wine, particularly drier reds, which are lower in sugar content than sweeter wines, such as white chardonnays. If you are going to drink hard alcohol, such as vodka, gin, tequila, or whiskey, avoid or limit mixed drinks that add sugar, such as daiquiris, piña coladas, margaritas, and so on. I mention this substitution because I know some people will consume alcohol even if I, and others, strongly advise against it. For those already struggling with depression, alcohol can cause and fuel depressive symptoms and should be avoided.

Instead of sodas and sugary "fruit juices" (many of which contain no juice or very little, but a lot of sugar), *swap with* organic juices containing 100 percent real juice. Or try kombucha, a drink that is made through the fermentation of sweet tea with a culture of yeast and good bacteria. Evidence shows that kombucha might help alleviate the symptoms of depression because of its healthy "Symbiotic Culture of Bacteria and Yeast" (SCOBY). This is a sort of gelatinous "raft" that floats on top of the kombucha brew, which seals off the kombucha from harmful outside bacteria and turns the sweet tea into a healthy, fermented brew.

Shopping Smart on a Budget

I recently had a conversation with a woman named Denise. She is married with three children, all under the age of eighteen. Her husband works for the city parks department, and she substitute teaches when she can pick up shifts.

Denise mentioned that eating healthy takes time, money, and energy. And in her household, those three things are precious commodities indeed. She noted that a single friend, who is a successful real estate agent, often tries to give her tips on where to shop, what to buy, and how to cook it.

But Denise made this excellent point: buying and cooking healthy foods can be both expensive and time consuming. So how do you eat "organic" (or close to it) when you are on a fixed budget? Admittedly, grocery stores that sell higher-end foods (i.e., health foods, organic foods, and produce) can be pricier. So here are some tips if, like Denise, your budget and schedule make it more difficult to eat fresh, healthier foods:

- **Make your local farmer's market a weekly experience.** You may be surprised at the deals you can find at the farmer's market. While you have to be careful, as some specialty items can be pricey, you can also find great deals on fresh, bulk veggies there (such as carrots and other items in season). Bring the kids or a friend and make it an outing.
- **Do the time-consuming prep work on the weekend.** While not everyone has time to prep their meals on any given Saturday, what with kids' swim meets, Mommy and Me classes, or orchestra performances, this can also be a great way to teach your little ones their way around the kitchen. Then refrigerate or freeze the fresh-made meals, saving midweek prep time and energy.
- **Use labor-saving technology.** Do what your grandmother did: find whatever is fresh around the kitchen and throw it into the Crock-Pot or pressure cooker (such as an Instant Pot) before you leave for the day. Add chicken or beef or your protein of choice. (Also, you can buy chickens whole to save money.)
- **Look for deals.** You can use your local supermarket's phone app or the old-fashioned standby: coupons from mailers or the paper. Some supermarkets will reduce their days-old produce and place it in a sales section (typically at the back of the store). While the store can't keep it, it's still perfectly edible—just eat it right away or freeze it.
- **Keep a record of how many meals you eat out.** Try doing this for one month. You might be surprised at how much

cash goes toward that "occasional" fast-food meal. Then set a monthly budget for eating out, and make it a once-a-week treat for everyone. Also, nowadays, you can actually find healthy foods at fast-food restaurants (salads, grilled chicken, and so on).

- **Watch for cost-saving opportunities at discount warehouse stores.** While big-box stores such as Sam's Club and Costco can suck the money right out of your wallet, you can also find great bulk deals on healthy items. Shop just for produce or fresh staples rather than getting seduced by that new 120-inch flat-screen TV.
- **Grow your own vegetables or fruits in a backyard plot or container garden.** Even if you live in the Snowbelt, or in an apartment, you can time your growing season and utilize window boxes or other indoor growing ideas.

Health and Hydration

Amid our discussion of beneficial foods, let's not overlook one of the most essential components of nutrition: water. Ever since you were in grade school, you've heard that H_2O is an indispensable element of the earth's ecosystem, necessary for sustaining every aspect of life—plants, trees, animals, oceans, weather systems, and human beings. Water, of course, is also an indispensable element for our individual bodies if we hope to survive and thrive.

In the United States, there is little risk that you will not *survive* because of lack of water . . . but it's that second word we can focus on: *thrive*.

Scientists have identified a strong connection between dehydration and depression, noting that even mild dehydration will affect your moods. Two studies from the Human Performance Laboratory at the University of Connecticut demonstrate that it takes relatively little dehydration (1.5 percent loss in the body's normal water volume) to alter your energy level, mood, and ability to think clearly.[5] The study also found that consuming water has a "significant impact" on alleviating depression and supporting mental sharpness. It can also help with sleep disorders. One of the study's lead researchers, Lawrence E. Armstrong, professor of physiology in UConn's Department of Kinesiology, found that when the subjects were dehydrated, they were more irritable and fatigued. According to Dr. Armstrong, not drinking enough water can also cause headaches, sleepiness, and confusion.

Numerous similar scientific studies support the UConn hydration report, identifying the many benefits of adequate water consumption. Nutrition expert Kathleen M. Zelman enumerates some of the benefits of proper hydration.[6] Water intake helps to . . .

- **Balance body fluids.** Bodily fluids help to support digestion, absorption, circulation, creation of saliva, transportation of nutrients, and body-temperature regulation.
- **Support weight loss.** For many years, water consumption has been recognized as an effective weight-loss strategy. Water is a zero-calorie method for helping yourself feel full so you'll eat less food. Also, water serves as a replacement for other beverages that contain calories and perhaps unhelpful ingredients.
- **Maintain muscle mass.** Cells that don't sustain the proper balance of fluids and electrolytes cause muscle fatigue. That's why drinking ample fluids during exercise is essential. The American College of Sports Medicine recommends that people consume about seventeen ounces of fluid about two hours before exercise. During exercise, you should drink fluids at regular intervals to replace fluids lost through perspiration.

- **Sustain kidney function**. Fluids are responsible for moving waste throughout the body. Blood urea nitrogen is the chief waste product. It dissolves in water and thus can easily move through the body and the kidneys, where it is released into urine. A sign your body is properly hydrated can be found in the urine. When you've had enough fluids, urine will be odorless and light in color. If your body has not received the fluids it needs, the kidneys retain fluid for other purposes, and urine has a more concentrated color and odor.
- **Aid digestion**. Sufficient hydration allows proper flow along your gastrointestinal tract and decreases possible constipation. When fluids are inadequate, the colon takes water from stools to provide hydration, and constipation is the result.

So how much water consumption will help you thrive? You've probably heard the mantra that you should drink at least eight eight-ounce glasses of water each day (i.e., sixty-four ounces). Well, there is a lot of truth to that. Don't forget that our bodies are composed of approximately 60 percent water. We need a lot of water to keep our biological machine humming along in good health.

Actually, I believe we all need a bit more water than that, depending upon body weight. What I advise my clients is that they drink the equivalent of half their body weight in ounces of water each day. For example, if you weigh 176 pounds, you should drink 88 ounces per day—that's the equivalent of eleven eight-ounce glasses of water. The trick is to start early in the morning and have a water container near you during the day—even while you are driving.

And just to be clear: I am talking about *water*, not just *liquids*. So if you have juice or coffee with lunch, don't count those ounces toward your daily water intake. Remember that a lot of the liquids we rely on each day—coffee, soda, black tea, beer—contain either caffeine or alcohol, both of which are diuretics. In other words, they actually do the *opposite* of what water does: they dehydrate you rather than hydrate you.

Your Personal Action Plan

My goal in this chapter has been to give you a "mountaintop" view of how a well-balanced, nutritious diet leads to better health in general and relief from depression in particular. Let's look at some concrete steps you can take to improve your diet.

1. **Take the two-week food log challenge.** Many of us are quite surprised to discover what we *really* eat, as opposed to what we *think* we are putting into our bodies. Carefully track what you've been eating to help you spot areas for improvement and create better habits as you change your diet. This first step will give you (and your health professional) a good idea of where you are now, so you will know what you need to do to improve your health.

2. **Conduct an inventory of your refrigerator and pantry to see how many foods you own that have sugars or sweeteners added.** How can you cut down on these foods, as well as on sugars and sweeteners? Make a list of your favorite sugary foods and drinks, and research alternatives to each one.

3. **Be extra vigilant on your upcoming shopping trips.** The next time you go to the grocery store, stock up on alternative food and drinks that don't contain added sugar.

4. **Lean on a support system.** Getting healthy takes help—reach out to a friend or relative who can serve as an accountability partner. Check in with this person daily for one week and communicate how you are doing on the items listed in this chapter.

5. **After four weeks on your new nutritional regimen, stop and intentionally evaluate how different you feel.** If you have made significant modifications to your nutrition and hydration, you've probably noticed changes along the way. But after a month's duration, carefully assess your energy level, your mental sharpness, your sleep quality, and especially your mood.

CHAPTER 11

Time to Take Out the Trash

Detox Your Body of Pollutants to
Improve Your Overall Wellness

As a sixth-grade teacher, Katinna loved her students. But by the time summer vacation rolled around, she couldn't wait to lock up her classroom in Whittier, California. At the end of the school year, she packed her belongings and her cat and began the eleven-hundred-mile drive to her mom's house in Seattle. She had planned on staying just a few weeks. Little did she know she would spend half her summer there, some days barely getting out of bed.

Katinna's depression had been an intermittent nemesis in her life since her midteens. Lately, however, familiar symptoms like fatigue and emotional numbness had intensified, and new symptoms had shown up, including stomach cramps and acid reflux.

For Katinna, getting through the school year had been a major challenge. Despite being a devoted and conscientious teacher, she had to admit that oftentimes she hadn't been fully present for her students.

After her scheduled two weeks with her mom, Katinna felt too tired to return home and extended her stay in Seattle. And that's when something occurred to her mother, Jeanine.

"Katinna, one of the women at my office experienced deep depression and health issues for years, but she did a program here in town, and it really helped her," Jeanine said. "Maybe we should talk to her."

Katinna was still sitting in the corner of the couch where she'd spent most of the morning. She asked, "And she's not depressed anymore?"

"She says she feels great."

Katinna suddenly felt hopeful for the first time she could remember. "Okay, let's call her," she said.

Depression can be debilitating because some symptoms (like fatigue or low energy) increase the difficulty of daily life, while other symptoms (like hopelessness or disengagement) sabotage the motivation for even trying. It's a double dose of hardship that affects every area of life. Plus, depression is linked to so many contributing factors that getting to the root of what's really happening can be a challenge.

For example, the last thing Katinna would have imagined was that her depression and health issues were being fueled by something she was eating every day.

Catalysts That Create a Downward Spiral

When new clients seeking help with depression arrive, we always look for choices and behaviors that may be creating pollution in their bodies. And we often start with food.

There are chemicals and other substances in our environment—and particularly in the foods we eat—that can wreak havoc with the brain and neural system. These neurotoxins interfere with the electrical activities of nerve cells, impair cellular communication, and shorten the life span of those cells. The results can be devastating. In fact, neurotoxins have been linked to brain tumors, Alzheimer's disease, migraines, chronic fatigue, ALS, insomnia, inflammation, brain fog, memory loss, bloating, fatigue, thyroid dysfunction, kidney failure, soreness in the muscles and joints, and many other ailments.

Of particular importance to our many clients—and to you—is that neurotoxins are one of the most significant contributors to depression. We readily visualize the devastating impact of pollution on our environment—clogged streams, steaming landfills, billowing factory smokestacks, and polluted brown skies. Many of us feel impassioned and rally to clean up polluted landscapes. With that disturbing thought in mind, consider this: we must learn to apply the same intensity and motivation in regard to the destruction taking place in our own polluted bodies.

Where Do Toxins Come From?

The most common way you and I get toxins into our bodies is through things that we ingest, inhale, or absorb from our diets or our environments. So, let's first discuss what people typically consume, and in particular what depressed people consume. I am not going to send you on a guilt trip about eating hamburgers and ice cream . . . but my point is extremely important if you want to heal your depression. In essence, as I pointed out in the previous chapter, good food produces a good mood; bad food produces a bad mood. I know this sounds simple, but it's so true! To the degree that you strengthen and support your physical health, you will also strengthen and support your mental health.

As you know, the standard American diet consists largely of high-sugar, highly processed, chemically enhanced substances brimming with neurotoxins. In fact, there are so many chemicals in our food that some things we eat every day have been banned in other countries for being unsafe. Certain artificial food dyes, for example, are banned in some countries because they have been linked to cancer, allergies, and childhood hyperactivity. Even so-called "healthy" fare can be problematic. While we've all heard about the benefits of wild-caught salmon, farm-raised salmon is another story and is banned in Australia and New Zealand. This is because farm-raised salmon are often fed a diet filled with anti-biotics. Farm-raised fish can also have higher levels of pollutants that have been linked with elevated stroke risks for women. And brominated vegetable oil (BVO) has been banned in more than a hundred countries, yet it is commonly used as an emulsifier in citrus-flavored sodas and sports drinks in America.

How often are we ingesting toxins that damage our bodies and brains? For most of us, that answer is *daily*, especially if we frequently eat or drink the following:

- foods that contain additives such as artificial preservatives, food colorings, artificial thickeners, and/or a variety of chemicals
- chemical sweeteners, including Nutrasweet, Equal, Spoonful, and any other artificial sweetener found in processed foods or drinks
- processed foods and snacks including things made with refined carbohydrates, refined grains, and white flour
- any fried foods
- fish from rivers or lakes with high levels of mercury
- fruits and vegetables grown with the use of pesticides and herbicides (In fact, the Environmental Working Group has identified twelve fruits and vegetables consistently regarded as the most contaminated. I'll tell you more about the "Dirty Dozen" and "Clean Fifteen" fruits and vegetables in your personal action plan at the end of this chapter.)

In addition to ingesting toxins in and on our food, you and I are exposed to toxins every day in our homes and environments. Inhaling or absorbing chemicals from household cleaning products, glues, carpets, and smog can expose us to neurotoxins too, as can microwaving food in plastic containers, eating food cooked in aluminum foil, or cooking in nonstick pans that are allowed to get too hot.

Sometimes people are exposed to harmful toxins when they abuse drugs and illicit substances, especially ecstasy, LSD, cocaine, and marijuana. Alcohol is also neurotoxic, and studies have long associated heavy drinking with brain damage, including harm to cells responsible for our thoughts, emotions, and movements, along with harm to the supporting glial cells.[1] How much alcohol does it take to damage the brain? Research studies have suggested differing quantities, especially since individuals respond differently to alcohol consumption. One study analyzed the impact of alcohol on the brains of 550 men over a thirty-year period and concluded that individuals who had roughly one drink a day—an average of four to six beers or five to seven glasses of wine per week—were *three times more likely* to experience brain atrophy than those who didn't drink.[2]

Finally, as Katinna was about to discover, sometimes food allergies or sensitivities can set up inflammation and reactions in the body that can be just as devastating as the damage caused by the toxins described above.

Celiac disease, inflammation from gluten, and inflammation from other foods such as dairy products and sugar are all major contributors to depression. Lactose intolerance and fructose malabsorption, other dietary intolerances, are also big offenders, as they contribute to deficiencies of the essential amino acid L-tryptophan. These deficiencies have been linked to clinical depression, anxiety, and ADHD.

Katinna was ready to learn more. At her urging, her mother contacted Bree, a colleague from work, and invited her over on a

Saturday morning to meet Katinna and talk about her experiences with depression—and the food that had been fueling it.

Bree had come to us two years earlier, desperate for help. Depressed and plagued by headaches, fatigue, and chronic stomach upset, Bree had spent years looking for solutions. Shortly after we started Bree on a gluten-free diet, her depression began to lift. Before long, most of her other symptoms disappeared as well.

Bree was more than happy to meet with Katinna and her mother to share her story. She talked about making the life-changing discovery that she was gluten intolerant and how unknowingly eating the wrong kinds of foods had contributed for years to her depression.

Katinna had a lot of questions. She was skeptical at first, but the more she learned, the more hope she began to feel.

What's the Big Deal about Gluten?

In recent years, it seems the word *gluten* shows up every time we turn around. Gluten-free products line the aisles of our grocery stores. Gluten-free menu items are now available at our favorite restaurants. Why is it that so many people these days need to free themselves from gluten?

Gluten is a protein found in wheat, barley, and rye. Chances are, you have heard of celiac disease and gluten intolerance. These are two different responses the body can have to the gluten protein. While both conditions have similar symptoms, they represent different reactions occurring in the body. Celiac disease is an autoimmune condition in which the immune system attacks the lining of the small intestine. While gluten on its own isn't damaging the body of someone with celiac disease, it is the catalyst that causes the body to attack itself. Non-celiac gluten sensitivity, on the other hand, occurs when the body views gluten as an invader and uses inflammation in and around the digestive tract to fight back.

The first symptoms of gluten sensitivity are often related to the digestive tract and include gas, bloating, diarrhea, and constipation. All of that sounds unpleasant enough, but there are even more associated difficulties. People with gluten sensitivities often experience brain fog, mental or physical fatigue, and dizziness. Sometimes they are diagnosed with autoimmune diseases including Hashimoto's thyroiditis, lupus, or multiple sclerosis.

Here is another common symptom of gluten sensitivity: depression. In fact, one placebo-controlled study compared participants' depression scores while on diets designed to isolate sensitivities to gluten and whey.[3] The findings showed that 90 percent of participants who ate gluten reported feeling more depressed than those who were given the placebo.[4] It's also interesting that the study identified feelings of depression that had been induced by *short-term exposure to gluten*. In other words, if you are sensitive to gluten, it doesn't take a lifetime of eating the wrong things to make you feel depressed—it can happen right away.

The point is, if your diet is creating neurotoxicity, inflammation, or other potentially dangerous reactions in your body, it's no wonder you are depressed. Furthermore, it is time to make a change. You *can* regain control of your life, your moods, and your health—and it starts one bite at a time.

Rarely a day goes by that we don't hear or read something about the importance of clean eating. And there's a great reason for that! Ridding your diet of pollutants and poisons is a foundational part of improving your mood and your health.

How to Start Detoxing Your Body

The body has multiple organs and systems—the liver, kidneys, lymphatic system, lungs, and skin—that work together to filter and flush toxins out of your body.

Unfortunately, these organs and systems can become overwhelmed by the large amounts of toxins in our diets and environment encountered each day. To make matters worse, unless we are very intentional about diet and lifestyle, there's a good chance we're not supporting these organs and systems with the nutrition and activities they need to stay in tip-top shape.

When we see a new client who is struggling with depression, I often recommend a three-week protocol designed to cleanse and detox the body. The protocol incorporates detox agents, dietary changes, and actions that support the body in performing at maximum capacity—eliminating problem-causing toxins that are affecting health and mood. Here is the protocol that I recommend.

Detox Agents

Every day, do at least two of these:

- Drink a cup of dandelion root tea in the morning and another one in the afternoon.
- Take 500 mg of N-acetyl cysteine (NAC) twice a day.
- Take 300 mg of milk thistle (extracted from the fruit or seed, not the leaf, and standardized to 70 to 80 percent of the active ingredient silymarin).

Dietary Changes

- Eliminate *all* alcohol, soda, energy drinks, coffee, and juices or teas with added sugar.
- Avoid all candy and other sweets.
- Drink two cups or more of fresh-pressed vegetable juice every day.
- Limit animal products; eat no more than six ounces of animal flesh a day.
- Avoid all dairy products except for butter.

- Focus on whole foods (whatever you can buy in the produce section).
- Drink at least two liters of water a day.

Moving the Blood and Lymphatics

Every day, do at least two of the following:

- Dry skin brushing, which involves brushing your skin with a soft brush prior to a bath or shower. This provides gentle exfoliation, boosts circulation, and encourages new cell growth.
- Spend time in a sauna, then follow up with a cold rinse for ninety seconds or less. (I recommend choosing this at least three times a week.)
- Exercise for at least twenty to thirty minutes at a time. Exercise boosts circulation through the body, which helps flush toxins out.

Sleep

Get at least seven and a half hours of sleep a night. This not only will help you feel rested and less stressed; sleep reduces inflammation so the body can function at its best.

If you decide to follow the protocol for yourself, in addition to helping your body get rid of built-up toxins, this plan will also eliminate foods—gluten, corn, soy, dairy, eggs, and sugar—that are common causes of food sensitivities and inflammation in the body. What this means is that, after following this protocol for three weeks, you are in the perfect position to slowly reintroduce common problem foods back into your diet, paying close attention to any reactions you may be having.

Pick one of the foods that was eliminated—bread, for example—and eat it twice a day for two days. Keep a journal and write down any differences you notice in your body, energy, or mood. Do you feel more depressed? Have headaches or joint pain? Feel bloated or fatigued? Are you experiencing brain fog or trouble concentrating?

If your body responds negatively to that food, remove it again from your diet. Wait a few days, then reintroduce a different food and pay attention to how your body responds.

Whether you have gluten sensitivities or not, when it comes to managing your mood, clean eating is going to make a major difference.

A New Lease on Life

Katinna listened intently as Bree shared her story. She could relate to much of what Bree had experienced in terms of physical symptoms, emotional struggles, and frustration at not finding ready answers.

Things that Bree shared about food also rang a bell for Katinna, who loved breads and pasta. Katinna had always counted herself lucky for being able to eat whole wheat bagels for breakfast, sandwiches made with multigrain breads for lunch, and pasta for dinner without putting on weight. Now she wondered if her ability to eat all the grains she wanted had been more of a bane than a blessing.

In theory, hearing the similarities between her experiences and Bree's might have been discouraging. In reality, Katinna felt just the opposite. She felt relieved to know that a diagnosis might be around the corner and hopeful that if something had helped Bree to feel better physically and emotionally, it could help Katinna as well. Bree had a healthy glow and level of enthusiasm about her that Katinna had longed to experience in her own life, and for the first time in a long time, she began to believe it was possible.

That night as she got ready for bed, Katinna felt peaceful and excited at the same time. She couldn't wait to take the steps to reclaim her life. As she drifted off to sleep, she thought of the new class of sixth graders she would get to meet as soon as school began again. It would be great to be back.

Your Personal Action Plan

All the knowledge in the world about ridding your body of debilitating toxins and poisons won't do you a bit of good unless you begin today taking control of what you put in your body. Here are five things you can start doing right away:

1. **Decrease the amount of pesticides you ingest by buying organic fruits and vegetables or by choosing produce from the "Clean Fifteen."** Even making the healthy choice to eat more fruits and vegetables can expose us to pesticides and herbicides. The EWG has identified twelve fruits and vegetables that are consistently the most contaminated, as well as fifteen consistently clean fruits and vegetables. Simply choosing fruits and vegetables that test lower in dangerous chemicals can drastically reduce exposure to pesticides.

   Here are the "Dirty Dozen" to avoid if you are unable to buy organic (eating nonorganic produce from this list will expose a person to an average of about fifteen pesticides a day): peaches, apples, sweet bell peppers, celery, nectarines, strawberries, cherries, pears, grapes, spinach, tomatoes, and potatoes.

   Here are the Clean Fifteen to enjoy (eating nonorganic produce from this list will expose a person to an average of about two pesticides a day): avocados, sweet corn, pineapples, cabbages, onions, sweet peas, papayas, asparagus, mangoes, eggplants, honeydew melons, kiwis, cantaloupes, cauliflower, and broccoli.

2. **Become a die-hard label reader.** The list of toxic substances in our food is long and growing. Here are some of the most common toxins to avoid, as well as where you are likely to find them:

- artificial colors: drinks, juice drinks, cereals, candy
- aspartame: NutraSweet, Equal, foods labeled "sugar free," diet soft drinks, chewing gum
- BHA and BHT: breakfast cereals, snack foods, processed meats
- calcium caseinate: protein supplements, energy bars
- diacetyl: butter flavoring on microwave popcorn
- high-fructose corn syrup: soda, teas, flavored drinks, juice drinks for kids, jellies, condiments
- monosodium glutamate: processed foods like potato chips, frozen dinners, lunch meat, and salad dressing
- nitrites and nitrates: cured meats, including hot dogs and lunch meats
- potassium bromate or bromated flour: breads, bakery goods, tortillas
- sucralose: foods and drinks made with Splenda
- trans fats: bakery items, frozen pizza, snack foods, frozen meals

3. **Give rebounding a try.** Rebounding involves steady, gentle jumping on a trampoline or rebounder, as the mini trampolines are often called. As you jump up and down, the gravitational pull is believed to create circulation in your lymphatic system, flushing toxins from your body and boosting your immune system, blood flow, and digestion.

4. **Make green smoothies your new best friend.** Fruits and vegetables have great detoxing properties, and many of them are

perfect ingredients for a healthy morning smoothie. Be sure to include some of the following: green apples, green leafy vegetables, flaxseed, hemp seeds, avocado, lemons, oranges, limes, green tea.

5. **Start your day with a tall glass of lemon water.** Lemon water helps flush toxins, improves digestion, fights germs and bacteria, and provides you with vitamin C, which your body needs to produce collagen for younger looking skin.

CHAPTER 12

Is Your Gut Stuck in a Rut?

The Little-Known Power of Psychobiotics to Relieve Depression

Two Decembers, exactly 130 years apart, helped define the face of the European continent we know today.

In the summer of 1812, French emperor Napoleon Bonaparte assembled the largest army ever gathered in the history of the world up to that point. In June 1812, more than six hundred thousand men took part in the invasion of Russia. Just six months later, an army only one-sixth that size had escaped—defeated, starving, and demoralized.

Fast-forward to 1942, and once again, Russia was center stage in an epic clash of massive armies. This time, it was Hitler and the Nazi army that invaded the Soviet Union, hoping to gain valuable territory for the Third Reich. Having left Germany the previous June, by early December 1942, the German force was nearly defeated.

In both cases—Bonaparte and Hitler—a major factor in their military failures in Russia came down to a simple fact: there just wasn't enough food.

Quoting Frederick the Great, essayist and philosopher Thomas Carlyle famously wrote in 1866, "An Army, like a serpent, goes upon its belly."[1]

Both Hitler and Bonaparte learned this fact quite bitterly, standing by helplessly as their armies languished, strung out along weak supply lines deep in the heart of Russia.

Not dissimilarly, the mental and physical health of a person marches on the health of their gut. There are billions of tiny "soldiers" in your stomach. Thriving, healthy bacteria lead to healthy living, while starved or decimated bacteria can lead to unhealthy living, malaise, and disease.

Even more intriguing, however, are new discoveries linking the health of your gut with the treatment of depression. An emerging body of research has linked mental health with the gut microbiome— the technical term for the one hundred trillion or so "good" bacteria that live inside your digestive system. These good bacteria have been shown to affect everything from your digestive health to your heart functions to your immune system.

This area of study has proven so significant to our understanding of human health that in 2007 the National Institutes of Health launched the Human Microbiome Project. This ambitious study is one of several international efforts designed to collect and make available staggering amounts of data regarding the microbiota and their relationship to various diseases. And, most exciting for our purposes, the activity of these bacteria has been shown to have a significant influence on the activity of the brain itself, including the function and dysfunction of neurotransmitters that affect our moods.

This area of research—which has led some to call the gut the second or "little" brain—isn't entirely new. It started with a more complete picture of the neuron network in the lower regions of the body, which emerged in the late 1990s, when studies began to reveal that the enteric nervous system (ENS)—about one hundred million neurons embedded in the walls of our gut—had more power than its already-impressive handle on daily digestion and excretion.

To make it really simple: the vagus nerve is our body's biggest nerve, running from the brain down to the gut, where it branches into a vast information network of neurons. This two-lane highway, along with our immune system and hormones, is known as the gut-brain axis. Before, it was thought that this was for the brain to more closely monitor and control digestive functions, which is one of the most complex operations in the body.

But some studies have revealed that 90 percent of the fibers in the vagus nerve are actually sending messages *from* this intricate system of neurons *to the brain*, and not the other way around. Even more interesting is that the ENS uses more than thirty neurotransmitters, as many as the "big" brain uses, to send these signals, underscoring the relationship between the gut and mood disorders, which are typically related to the body's ability to produce, absorb, and use certain neurotransmitters such as serotonin.

What, then, is the origin of these messages sent through the vagus nerve? What is producing these neurotransmitters and communicating with our "big brains" along this two-lane highway?

According to the most recent studies in this exploding area of medicine, it turns out it's the bacteria of your gut microbiome, which significantly outnumber the densely packed ENS cells. For perspective, consider that the ENS has more nerves than the rest of your body combined, including the spinal cord. Wow.

You've undoubtedly heard the terms *antibiotic* and *probiotic* before, and we're going to talk about those a bit in this chapter. But first I want to introduce you to the most cutting-edge aspect of this research as it relates to depression. Coined by researcher and psychiatrist Ted Dinan at the University College Cork's Alimentary Pharmabiotic Centre in Ireland, the term *psychobiotics* specifically refers to strains of bacteria living inside your gut that can affect your mood.

That's right. Some of those tiny organisms send messages to your brain that directly influence your level of anxiety, happiness, satisfaction, and of course, depression.

Some of these psychobiotics alter your mood less directly. For example, certain strains are responsible for producing B vitamins, and as you've read a couple of times, B vitamins are critical for a healthy nervous system and for emotional well-being. For the first time in modern history, a wealth of medical research is supporting a view that the brain is not, in fact, the root of all mood disorders, and that opens up whole new avenues for treating depression and related disorders.

I attended a presentation recently where doctors learned about some of the latest discoveries on these fronts. There's so much data coming out, and it'll take time to process it all and then translate it into FDA-approved treatments, but the wheel is already turning. For example, for people who have a poor ecosystem of gut bacteria, researchers are doing stool transplants. Not the kind of topic you would want to discuss over dinner or on a first date, I realize, but it's an important area of exploration for depression relief. It's safer than medication with fewer side effects, it's very effective, and it's curing people of a multitude of illnesses and conditions all over the world. Already, US companies are paying for stool samples from healthy donors to be used in treatments.

While that route may be an option, what I'm hoping to do in this chapter is to help you change the course of your gut health long before that approach becomes necessary. There are other, simpler ways to support the presence of good bacteria and keep down the population of destructive strains, most importantly through adjusting your diet.

In chapter 10, we looked at an essential aspect of managing depression—proper nutrition. It's critical to avoid or mitigate some of the most destructive scenarios that affect our gut health. As you know, some foods are extremely beneficial to our overall health as well as our mental health. Likewise, some foods are detrimental, negatively affecting our moods. It's important to understand here that certain foods and even living organism supplements (probiotics and prebiotics) promote healthy gut bacteria. Those can go a long way toward healing your depression.

Maybe you're unsure if an unbalanced gut is actually one of the missing puzzle pieces in your quest to overcome depression. Let me tell you, almost every American has imbalances in their gut microbiome to some degree. It's unfortunately an inevitable side effect, we're learning, of our lifestyle and eating habits, especially the high-sugar and high-fat foods the average American consumes regularly.

According to experts studying the gut microbiome, the bacteria in your gut can be the "X factor" in what causes a genetic predisposition to emerge. In other words, your DNA may carry the possibility for you to have depression, and yet you may live most of your life depression free . . . until your gut population falls out of balance, turning your predisposition into a full-blown, chronic problem that a drug prescription won't fix.

Your Gut and Your Depression

Let's start off by making one thing absolutely clear: your gut and your brain are not separate. This matters because although we call depression a "mood disorder," it is an illness that goes much deeper than merely feeling sad or "blue."

In fact, a depression diagnosis conventionally means that your brain exhibits especially low levels of serotonin, the neurotransmitter responsible not only for happiness but also for things like sexual desire, memory, and the ability to sleep restfully. SSRIs (selective serotonin reuptake inhibitors) are what we've mostly used to treat depression because these drugs cause the brain to recirculate more serotonin instead of breaking it down.

But if mental illness is ultimately the result of imbalances in neurotransmitters in the brain, must we assume that the root causes of these imbalances, and therefore the focus of our solution, also rests in the brain? Absolutely not! At least, not anymore.

As I've suggested, the latest research shows us that what's going on in your gut influences what goes on in your brain—not the other way around. So, if the evidence shows us that the brain is responding to messages sent by the gut, primarily through the vagus nerve, then it makes sense to start at the root of the messages if we want a lasting solution.

Neurotransmitters and Hormones

If the network of neurons reaching between our brain, our gut, and the rest of our bodies is a highway, then the chemicals traveling along it may be thought of as mail trucks carrying messages from one part of the body to another. These mail trucks come in two basic varieties: neurotransmitters and hormones. These messengers have a lot in common, but there are some distinct differences worth noting.

Neurotransmitters are chemicals that travel through the nervous system and across the gaps between neurons to attach themselves to specific receptor sites. Hormones, also chemicals, are produced by the endocrine system (glands) and travel through the blood to interact with target organ cells. Both chemical types are intimately involved in regulating everything our bodies do consciously and subconsciously, including how we think and feel.

The primary chemical related to mood disorders is serotonin (a neurotransmitter), so anything that affects the body's ability to produce serotonin or keep more of it around for longer is going to have a serious impact on depression, including, and especially, when it's happening in the gut. Scientists have already discovered that oral ingestion of *Bifidobacterium infantis* (*B. infantis*) in test rats leads to increased levels of tryptophan, a critical ingredient in the manufacturing of serotonin; several other strains have been found to produce serotonin outright.

Likewise, when insufficiently produced in the brain, other chemicals associated with depression, like the neurotransmitter GABA, seem to lead to negative, obsessive thought patterns linked with depression. Researchers have found that certain gut microbes, including *Lactobacillus* and *Bifidobacterium* strains, actively secrete GABA.

Other bacteria produce the hormone norepinephrine and the neurotransmitter dopamine, two other chemicals you've likely heard of. These elements are associated with a host of bodily functions, including those impacted by depression, such as memory, alertness, motivation, arousal, and general feelings of well-being. Still other bacteria increase levels of oxytocin, the "feel good" hormone that washes through us when we experience positive physical contact like hugging or sex.

Besides bacteria that directly produce chemicals, some strains affect nerve cells like cannabinoid receptors. These receptors are involved in regulating mood and are often a cause in a vicious circle of contribution. Other receptors tell the brain through the vagus nerve to increase its production of GABA receptors (helpful when partner bacteria are secreting more of the stuff!).

So how does it help us to have more serotonin and adjust the levels of other mood-regulating chemicals in the gut when it's a deficiency in the brain that causes depression? Evidence suggests that by using the vagus nerve, the gut microbiome can let the brain know you have plenty of the neurotransmitters needed to produce a good mood and combat depression. Even more, the brain will actually respond as if those chemicals were flooding its own neural pathways.

This is exciting news for our ability to treat depression more naturally. It could mean that we need only focus on supporting the healthy growth of specific bacteria, rather than introducing medications with harmful side effects. And if the brain's ability to produce or absorb the neurotransmitters is damaged, the gut may be able to intervene.

Inflammation and Stress

I find it frustrating that common treatment approaches haven't changed much in the last several decades, even though our understanding of depression has. The most advanced medical communities now consider many psychiatric illnesses (including depression) to be immunological and related to chronic high levels of inflammation, which alters the landscape significantly. It shouldn't be so surprising since we know many chronic and degenerative diseases arise when we have a weakened or malfunctioning immune system.

We touched on the topic of inflammation and depression in chapters 4 and 11, but let's expand on that discussion for our exploration of psychobiotics and a healthy gut. Inflammation is the process by which our immune system, especially our white blood cells, protects us from infection. A certain amount of inflammation can be normal and positive. Sometimes, however, the immune system inappropriately triggers an inflammatory response when we're healthy, or it overreacts to an infection, causing the body to damage itself instead of protecting itself.

For example, studies of the gut microbiome reveal a condition called "leaky gut syndrome," in which the intestinal wall allows certain substances to leak into the bloodstream where they don't belong. This puts the immune system on alert, creating inflammation in the gut and subsequently in the brain.

Adding to the problem is another process known as "serotonin steal," which happens when inflammation in the gut causes the microbiota to divert tryptophan away from the brain. As we've already discussed, tryptophan is a key ingredient used to make serotonin— less tryptophan means less serotonin. In fact, observations of this process reveal subjects' experiences of increased anxiety, insomnia, and depression.

So one school of thought goes like this: heal the inflammation, heal the immune system, and you'll heal the psychiatry. With more than 70 percent of our immune system based in the gut and regulated by gut bacteria, it's clear this region of our body and its collective of microorganisms steer the ship of our health. People with upset in the gut microbiome may even experience an increased number of colds and flus.

I don't find it coincidental that depression has long been linked to weak immune systems and a higher frequency of illness. Nor is it a coincidence that, perhaps more than any other approach we take at the Center, restoring balance to the gut microbiome restores good health throughout the body, from head to toe.

As we saw in chapter 4, a discussion of inflammation necessarily includes a discussion of stress, one of the biggest known causes of chronic inflammation. It's also well known that stress and depression are intimately related—not just in the obvious way that living with depression can cause stress and vice versa, but also because studies have shown that people with chronic depression often have elevated levels of cortisol in their systems. Cortisol is a chemical our bodies release in direct response to stress.

What most people don't know is that certain strains of bacteria reduce cortisol levels, which decreases stress, and therefore in turn decreases depression. A 2015 study indicates a lot of promise from the introduction of certain bacteria to the gut to relieve stress and anxiety, specifically by reducing the output of cortisol.

"This study represents a proof of principle," said Dr. Gerard Clarke, who presented the study's findings at the Society for Neuroscience 2015 Annual Meeting. "The question we are asking now is, can we advance this further and can we use these psychobiotics to deal with the stressors that we encounter on the roller coaster of life, or develop further psychobiotics for patients with stress-related disorders such as depression or anxiety?"[2]

The answer to that question has yet to be fully vetted by our accepted systems of medical practice. As far as we here at The Center are concerned, however, the answer will undoubtedly be yes!

A Delicate Balancing Act

Though still too new to draw productive conclusions regarding diagnoses and treatment, mounting evidence proves that major changes to our gut microbiomes occur as early as our first breaths. These changes are due to differences in the bacteria we're exposed to when we experience a natural vaginal birth versus Cesarean birth. Moreover, early-life stress such as an infant's or child's separation from his or her mother—a known risk factor for major depression in adulthood—causes even more changes that can throw our gut microbiomes out of balance.

So imbalances start at birth and continue to plague us as part of the natural aging process. That's right, the ecosystem of one hundred trillion bacteria in the body naturally becomes less diverse each day as strains emerge, die, struggle, or thrive. But we can certainly compound the problem through a poor diet, overuse of antibiotics, and more. Even excessive hygiene can mess with this living formula-in-flux.

So we have all these strains of bacteria that are supposed to be in the gut living in a particular, delicate balance to keep us well. Anything that upsets this balance, including the introduction or unchecked growth of "unhealthy" bacteria or the dying off of too many "good" bacteria, can then affect the messages that are being sent to our brains. This, in turn, affects the messages our brains send to other parts of the body. But just as we can cause imbalance through the choices we make, we can restore balance through making new, different choices.

It all sounds so simple, but there are some complications. A major problem in connecting gut imbalances to the health issues you're currently experiencing is that the effect is not always immediate. For example, one study found that while some routine antibiotic treatments created "profound and rapid" changes within just three days, some test subjects' microbiomes had only partially returned to normal four years after treatment.[3]

The good news is that while the causes for gut imbalances are many, it's relatively easy to restore balance through proper dietary supplements; in many instances, it doesn't even matter what caused the imbalance in the first place. That said, prevention is always the best medicine, so I want you to understand both how to resolve dysbiosis—a microbial imbalance or maladaptation inside the body— and also how to prevent it from becoming a recurring problem.

Antibiotics

According to the Centers for Disease Control (CDC), for every one thousand people, approximately eight to nine hundred antibiotics are dispensed. At this rate—and our consumption of these drugs in the United States is shrinking compared to developing nations—it's not surprising that at least two million people annually suffer infections from antibiotic-resistant strains of bacteria.

You might argue that antibiotics are critical to health care and resistance is an unfortunate side effect, and you would be right . . . mostly. The problem is that the CDC has also determined that nearly 50 percent of antibiotic use in US hospitals is unnecessary or inappropriate. This means we are unnecessarily creating a massive potential for disease outbreaks and a declining effectiveness of antibiotic treatment. Why? Because as we overuse and misuse antibiotics, certain diseases become resistant to the drugs, thus causing a proliferation of those specific diseases.

The politics of antibiotic use and overuse aside, the fact remains that with so many people taking antibiotics, we're looking at the biggest cause of upset to the gut microbiome. It's part of the reason I said earlier that almost all Americans suffer from gut imbalance to some degree. While we may be healing certain illnesses through antibiotic use, we are also undoubtedly setting the stage for more to arise.

Think of how an antibiotic works: you ingest this substance, and it goes after infection-causing bacteria like a bloodhound, then eliminates them from your system. The problem is that many antibiotics, especially broad-spectrum treatments, are more like bloodhounds with crop dusters. They hunt down those "bad" bacteria all right, but when it comes to elimination, they indiscriminately take out a lot of good bacteria as well.

The most aggressive antibiotics can damage your system so thoroughly that some good strains of bacteria can't even grow back—sometimes not for years, and sometimes not at all, without being intentionally reintroduced.

Perhaps you already know it's fairly common for a person taking a round of antibiotics to develop a yeast infection afterward. What's happening is that the antibiotic has killed off so many good bacteria, *Candida* strains (yeast) thrive and take over. Their reproduction is out of control. The resulting infection is evidence of gut imbalance at work.

We see a particularly large number of female clients who have suffered from recurring yeast infections, often after taking antibiotics; the vast majority have never had a health care professional link this routine to their depression. If you've ever had a yeast infection, that's just one very common sign that your body has suffered from an imbalance in the gut microbiome. And it's possible—in fact, likely—that you've never fully recovered.

If we accept that taking antibiotics can lead to a gut imbalance, then we have to account for this and be much more proactive whenever we take these medications. It's fairly common for doctors to alert patients to potential digestive side effects like diarrhea, but they don't often take the conversation further. The latest research linking gut imbalances to mood disorders will, I hope, change that soon. Until it does, you can become more vigilant about your use of antibiotics, taking them only when absolutely necessary, and supporting their use with prebiotics and probiotics.

Prebiotics and Probiotics

Prebiotics are substances that support the growth of certain microbiota, while probiotics are made up of the microorganisms themselves. Just one probiotic supplement contains billions of good bacteria. Introducing probiotics to resolve issues means you're attempting to restore proper levels of intestinal microflora for proper digestion and absorption of nutrients.

In turn, prebiotics and probiotics help rein in harmful strains of bacteria that would otherwise overpopulate if growth were left unchecked, even preventing and inhibiting infections. Unlike probiotics, prebiotics are not microorganisms—they are nondigestible and typically nonabsorbable nutrients that help good bacteria grow and flourish. Most prebiotics are fibers or carbohydrates that can be taken as supplements or found occurring naturally in foods.

When it comes to balancing the gut, you can't do it quickly. Remember, we're talking about living organisms. It may be helpful to think of the gut as a garden of sorts—we want to cultivate more of the bacteria we need and weed out the kind we don't want. Just like with a garden, first you have to create an ideal environment that supports healthy growth of whatever it is you're planting. In this case, we're talking about prebiotics as the "good soil" with lots of rich fertilizer, and probiotics as the "good seed."

It's important to understand how probiotics are absorbed in the body. First, not all types can survive the journey through your stomach and large intestine. And second, others tend to "leak" out into the bloodstream. For probiotic treatment to be useful, the microbiota must get where they're intended to go. Many supplement types have no real effect (besides as a placebo), because the strains don't ever make it past your stomach acid. This is why it's critical to rely on good research and, ideally, to work with professionals. They will help you determine precisely which strains you might need and which brands of supplements will be most effective to address your unique concerns and medical history.

It's also important to understand that not all probiotics are created equal. Some probiotics will give better results than others, so it is critical to validate that a particular probiotic is effective and will work for you. Here are some criteria for evaluating a probiotic supplement to make sure it best fits your needs:

- **Select a probiotic that contains a prebiotic (fiber/food for the probiotic).** This is an important component of any quality probiotic supplement as it will be essential in ensuring that the probiotic survives the journey into the digestive system. Think of it as taking a long trip and packing some snacks for the ride.
- **Use the correct potency.** When looking at a probiotic supplement, you will see the potency listed most often in "billions CFU." CFU stands for colony-forming units. Many manufacturers will suggest that the more billions, the better for you. But research clearly demonstrates that simply taking more is not necessarily better. The correct amount to take daily is between 10 and 20 billion CFU. Taking more will increase your cost while not providing any more benefits.[4]

Determine that the probiotic has a scientifically validated delivery system so the probiotic bacteria can survive exposure to stomach acid and bile, as well as making sure they are hydrated correctly and fed properly. Find a system that uses an all-natural method of delivering beneficial probiotic bacteria without chemicals and processing aids used in other systems, such as enteric coating, delayed release capsules, and pearls. Once you find a probiotic that looks suitable to your needs, conduct online research to discover its viability, or speak with a qualified nutritionist to get a recommendation.

But getting the right bacteria into your gut is a multifaceted task, involving more than pre-, pro-, and psychobiotics. Not surprisingly, it's the food and liquid we choose to put into our guts that will determine their long-term health. Our aim is to address gut imbalance and achieve the kind of balance that will lead to maximum health . . . including mental health.

Your Personal Action Plan

Before reading this chapter, you might have been familiar with information about gut health and psychobiotics . . . or completely unfamiliar! It can be a lot of terminology and explanation to take in. So to conclude our discussion of the topic, let's look at some simple and practical ways you can improve, enhance, and cultivate a healthy gut microbiome through the use of pre-, pro-, and psychobiotics.

1. **Do some research about what types of prebiotics, probiotics, and mood-improvement supplements might be best for you.** By no means am I trying to push our Center's products on you, but they are an option as well. Our team of experts has worked with a nutritional supplement company to produce a range of products that we believe are very helpful. Another option is to visit your trusted health-food

store—one that has a good nutrition section, preferably with a nutrition specialist on staff.

2. **Once you know the brands of the prebiotics, probiotics, and psychobiotics you want to buy, determine the right dosages for you.** I encourage you to consult your local naturopathic professional. If you do not have one close to you, then connect with one by phone or over the Internet.

3. **Determine to take your supplements for thirty days, and in a journal or the companion workbook to this book, record changes you notice in your mood and overall well-being.** Be mindful of the precautions and suggestions I have laid out in this chapter.

4. **If you can find a friend who will begin the journey with you, even better.** Two working together, encouraging and helping one another, are certainly better than one person trying to go solo. You can share your discoveries, discuss what is working for you to cause improvement, and keep each other accountable to sticking with the new regimen.

5. **After four weeks, revisit your original symptoms.** Have you seen a decrease in negative patterns or health problems? If so, how?

CHAPTER 13

The Magic of Micronutrients

Enjoy a Big Boost from Nutritional Supplements

Pete is a freelance graphic artist who enjoys working with clients all over the country. He never used to think of himself as an angry person, but over a span of five or six years, Pete had been feeling more isolated and irritated than ever before. Even worse, he found himself frequently annoyed with his wife, Sarah, and their twin sons, age ten.

Anger is a common symptom of depression in men and, sure enough, a family doctor diagnosed Pete with clinical depression and prescribed an antidepressant. After a few weeks, Pete felt that the pills hadn't helped at all and even seemed to make his foggy memory foggier, so he stopped taking the medication. His mood continued to decline.

A turning point for Pete took place one Saturday morning when he walked into the kitchen where Sarah and the boys were making French toast. They didn't see Pete immediately, which allowed him to watch unobserved from the doorway for several minutes.

The first thing he noticed was the laughter. One of the boys had dropped an egg on the kitchen floor, and the challenges of capturing the evasive yoke with a paper towel had both boys in stitches. Soon Sarah became so tickled by her boys' silliness that she too began laughing. Pete was taken aback . . . because he suddenly realized he hadn't heard his wife and kids laugh like that for months.

Just then, one of the boys spotted Pete in the doorway, nudged his brother, and they both stopped laughing and remembered something they needed to do in another room. And just like that, they were gone.

Pete looked at his wife. "What just happened?"

"They don't feel like being yelled at all the time." Sarah took a deep breath. "They're tired of getting your stern looks and harsh words. And so am I."

It was a wake-up call for Pete, who until that moment had been resigned to continue living in denial regarding his depression. He hadn't fully understood how his bad moods affected his family. They avoided him much of the time, and for good reason. He had turned into a world-class grump.

The next day Pete admitted to Sarah, "I need to do something. I get that. But I'm not a medication kind of guy—especially when I can tell that it's not even working."

After doing more research, the couple decided to seek help for Pete at The Center. The concept of whole-person care intrigued them, and when I immediately began to talk to them about getting Pete on specific, targeted supplements rather than prescriptions, they felt hopeful for the first time in a long time.

The Malnourished Brain

A depressed brain is often a malnourished brain.

Depression is frequently referred to as a chemical imbalance. But we also know that a depressed brain is often deficient in key nutrients and neurotransmitters. In chapter 10, we discussed the importance of healthy eating habits, and in this chapter we're exploring additional sources of nutrients. While diet alone does not improve depression, fortifying the brain with supplemental nutrients that replenish deficient levels is a helpful next step in your treatment plan.

Mark Hyman, MD, author of *The UltraMind Solution,* nailed it when he wrote, "What's remarkable is how backward the thinking about depression is. Doctors tend to only use vitamins *if* the antidepressants don't work. They should be prescribing the vitamins in the first place and then supplementing with antidepressants only *if* vitamins and lifestyle changes don't work."[1]

Dr. Hyman gives one kind of deficiency—a deficiency in folic acid—as an example, explaining, "If you have folate deficiency, it is unlikely that antidepressants will even work. . . . People with a low folate level have only a 7 percent response to treatment with antidepressants. Those with a high folate have a response rate of 44 percent. That's six times better. In medicine, if we get a 15 to 30 percent improvement we are happy; but a 600 percent improvement should be headline news."[2]

We have seen the same response over and over in our own clients. Supporting the brain with vitamins, minerals, and additional compounds in foods can influence neurotransmitters and affect mood. In addition, supplements can also result in less mental fog, less stress, and improved sleep. Finally, if an antidepressant turns out to be necessary, a well-supported brain is simply going to respond better than a malnourished brain.

In other words, when it comes to treating depression, supplements simply cannot be overlooked.

"Can't My Brain Get What It Needs from What I Eat?"

This is a common question, and one I hear often. My answer is yes and no. Our ancestors ate plenty of fresh fruit, plants, fish, and game—a diet that very likely supplied their brains with all the nutrients they needed.

As agriculture began, however, low-vitamin starches like wheat and corn became a regular part of people's diets. Nutrients in our diet continued to take a hit as advances in agriculture focused on improving crop traits like size, growth rate, and pest-resistance rather than nutrition. Plus, many modern farming techniques leave the soil depleted of important vitamins, minerals, and microbes, which results in plants with fewer nutrients.

The impact? One analysis of the nutrients in a dozen vegetables found that, between 1975 and 1997, average calcium levels dropped 27 percent, iron dropped 37 percent, vitamin A dropped 21 percent, and vitamin C dropped 30 percent. Other studies have found similar declines. In fact, according to Dr. Tim Lang, a professor at London's Centre for Food Policy, "You would have to eat eight oranges today to get the same amount of vitamin A your grandparents got from a single orange. And you would need to eat five to get the same level of iron."[3]

In addition to this disturbing decline, the average American continues to gravitate toward a diet made up largely of "fake food"—conglomerations of sugar, fat, and chemicals that take the concept of nutritional value to a new low.

So let's revisit the idea of getting all the nutrients you need from what you eat. Is it *possible*? In theory (and probably in practice for our ancestors), the answer is yes. Is it *probable* given the nutritional decline in our real food, plus our obsession with fake food? No.

The protocol we used with Pete is not unique. At The Center, we believe supplements and micronutrients are so foundational that every client who walks through our doors is evaluated for deficiencies, and most receive supplements to address problem areas.

What supplements should you consider as part of your whole-person approach to defeating depression? Before you begin taking any, I would recommend talking to your health care provider to determine which supplements are best for your needs, and what potential interactions (if any) they might have with any prescriptions you may be taking. Still, this list may serve as a good starting point for that discussion. I have organized a variety of supplements into categories based on their impact on mood, cognition, stress, and sleep. Much of this information is drawn from my collaboration with Redd Remedies, with whom I developed a line of supplements called Hope & Possibility. (You can find more information about Redd Remedies and the Hope & Possibility line at ReddRemedies.com.) [4]

Supplements to Lift Your Mood

When it comes to boosting mood, the following supplements can be very effective. Here are the supplements I recommend most often to achieve an overall lifting of the mood:

- **5-HTP** is a naturally occurring nutrient derived from the seed pods of the West African plant *Griffonia simplicifolia*. It acts as a precursor to the neurotransmitter serotonin, boosting levels in the brain. As a result, 5-HTP can improve mood, as well as relieve anxiety, depression, insomnia, and the urge to stress eat. Research also suggests that 5-HTP may ease some stress-related conditions such as PMS, migraines, and even fibromyalgia.
- **L-tyrosine** is an amino acid that acts as a precursor of the neurotransmitters norepinephrine and dopamine. When taken during times of low mood, it can boost energy and alertness, leading to depression relief.
- **Vitamin B_{12}** and **folic acid** play a role in producing brain chemicals that can affect cognition and mood. Regular consumption of B_{12} and folic acid not only reduces the risk of depression, it may also boost mental performance. But because these two nutrients work as a team, it's important to take them together.

- **Vitamin D** appears to work in the same way as many antidepressants by increasing levels of serotonin in the brain. Researchers from the University of Toronto, in a review of the effectiveness of vitamin D in treating mood disorders, found that vitamin D supplements administered during the winter months, when sunlight exposure is low, tended to improve mood.[5]

Supplements to Help You Think More Clearly

Many people who struggle with depression also struggle with mental confusion, detachment, forgetfulness, and a decreased ability to focus—often referred to as brain fog. This is why it's particularly important to support the depressed brain with habits and behaviors—like healthy eating, frequent exercise, and supplements—that improve cognition. The following supplements are a good place to start:

- **Vitamin B$_{12}$ and folic acid.** I mentioned these in the previous section, but they bear repeating here since low levels have been linked to poor cognitive performance, brain shrinkage, and even the development of Alzheimer's disease.
- **L-tyrosine** is linked with increased energy, alertness, and improved mood, as mentioned previously. It also improves mental focus. This was shown in a double-blind trial of twenty-three army personnel taking part in a weeklong combat training course. Those taking supplemental L-tyrosine found that it supported mental focus and mood while helping to prevent feelings of depression.[6]
- **Amla** is a popular Ayurvedic herb that's packed with antioxidants that can nourish the brain and improve mental functioning, including memory. Researchers are also looking into the herb's potential to clear beta-amyloid plaques and

slow the development of Alzheimer's disease and other neurodegenerative conditions.

- **Lion's mane** is a beautiful cascading mushroom that enhances cognition and memory by speeding myelination. Studies also show that lion's mane protects against brain cell death, which improves both mental clarity and memory. It has also been shown to halt the accumulation of beta-amyloid plaques, making it a possible treatment for those with Alzheimer's disease.
- **Magnesium L-threonate**, listed on supplement labels by its patented name Magtein, is a vital mineral for healthy brain biochemistry and a key ingredient (along with amla and lion's mane) in the Brain Awakening supplement we provide to our clients.[7] One recent study that appeared in the *Journal of Alzheimer's Disease* reported that supplementation with this unique form of magnesium helps to prevent brain atrophy and enhances brain fluidity in older adults.[8] It also has been shown to improve memory in those with dementia.

Supplements to Decrease Stress

There are some benefits to stress. Low-level stress, for example, boosts the production of brain chemicals that strengthen the connection between neurons, temporarily improving focus, memory, and learning. Stress can also motivate us to try harder, solve a problem, or change our priorities for the better.

But too much stress negatively impacts nearly every aspect of life, including our relationships, heart health, immunity, sleep, eating habits, and more. In fact, stress is almost always a contributing factor to depression.

According to Dr. Cindy Geyer of the True Health Initiative, the link between stress and depression is a strong one.[9] Some studies show that stress can suppress the growth of new neurons in the hippocampus, which is linked to depression. Stress causes inflammation in the body—also linked with depression.

Reducing and improving how you cope with stress can require a multifaceted approach. But, once again, supporting your brain and body with the right supplements provides a solid foundation for getting the results you need.

- **Holy basil** is an Ayurvedic adaptogen long used to counter stress. A growing body of preliminary research suggests that holy basil calms the brain and acts as a natural antianxiety agent and antidepressant, but without the potentially harmful side effects common to pharmaceuticals often used to treat depression and anxiety.
- **B vitamins** are critical for anyone experiencing chronic stress or anxiety. Vitamin B_1 boosts the immune system and improves the body's ability to handle stressful conditions. Vitamin B_3 is crucial in serotonin synthesis. Vitamin B_5 helps in modulating stress because of its relation to the adrenals.
- **Bacopa** may be best known for its brain-boosting benefits, but it also has been found to reduce anxiety and produce a feeling of calmness and tranquility. This is due to bacopa's ability to regulate the uptake of serotonin, to prevent dopamine receptor dysfunction, and to support the activity of GABA. As a bonus, bacopa also improves the quality of sleep.
- **Choline** is another well-known brain nutrient with mood benefits, and some studies suggest that supplementation may have a calming effect. Choline has also been shown to improve mania in people suffering from bipolar disorder.
- **GABA**, technically known as gamma-aminobutyric acid, is a nonessential amino acid that functions as a neurotransmitter, calming the brain by preventing too many neurons from firing at once. This essentially reduces brain activity and acts like a

brake during times of runaway stress. As a bonus, studies show that GABA enhances sleep and the production of endorphins, the feel-good brain chemicals that boost mood.

- **L-theanine**, an amino acid found in green tea, has a calming effect, reduces the physiological response to stress, and increases dopamine, serotonin, and the inhibitory neurotransmitter glycine. Studies show that L-theanine induces alpha brain wave activity in a dose-dependent manner, which makes people feel more relaxed without making them sleepy.

- **Magnesium** is the fourth most abundant mineral in the human body, yet it is readily depleted in the face of chronic stress. If you're low on magnesium anyway, stressful times can cause an even bigger deficit that, without intervention, can result in more stress, which depletes even more magnesium from your system.

- **Schisandra** has a long history of use as a mood lifter in traditional Chinese medicine. Because it increases dopamine levels in the brain, schisandra is often used to enhance focus and motivation. Studies have found that this ancient herb also restricts the amount of cortisol in the brain during times of stress.

Supplements to Improve Sleep

Problems getting to sleep (and staying that way) affect everyone from time to time. But when you're stressed or anxious, it's hard to shut off your thoughts, making sleep even more elusive. A full night's sleep contributes to not just physical health and energy but to your mental health and outlook as well. A quiet, calm, and dark sleep environment with a quality mattress is a great foundation for consistent and restorative sleep. A healthy diet, not eating too late, and calming yourself prior to bedtime (think meditation) are great contributors to ensuring quality sleep. The following herbs and nutrients can help as well:

- **California poppy** is a gorgeous orange wildflower packed with alkaloids that have sedative, analgesic, and antispasmodic benefits. Often used to treat insomnia, California poppy can also ease anxiety and nervous tension. One study that appeared in the journal *Planta Medica* found that California poppy acts to reduce anxious feelings under stressful conditions, and it does so safely.[10] Other research shows that it improves both the quality and the quantity of sleep without the "hangover" common to pharmaceutical sleep aids.

- **Hops** is best known as a major component in beer, but it also has a long history of medicinal use. According to a professor at the University of Extremadura in Badajoz, Spain, taking hops shortly before bedtime increases the activity of the neurotransmitter GABA.[11] This effectively decreases nocturnal activity in the circadian rhythm, normalizing the sleep/wake cycle and making it easier to get a good night's sleep.

- **Lemon balm** has long been used to improve nighttime calm. Lemon balm also boasts antianxiety benefits. In one double-blind, placebo-controlled study, healthy volunteers received either a standardized lemon balm extract or a placebo for seven days. By the end of the study, the researchers noted that the lemon balm supplement enhanced mood and significantly increased calmness.[12]

- **Magnesium** is the most effective relaxation mineral available, and it can improve your quality of sleep. This was shown in an eight-week double-blind, placebo-controlled trial of forty-six elderly volunteers suffering from insomnia. Those taking a magnesium supplement experienced an increase in the time spent sleeping as well as an uptick in the hormone melatonin compared to those taking a placebo. The participants taking the magnesium also reported falling asleep faster and experiencing fewer sleepless nights. Blood tests also found that they had lower cortisol levels, indicating less nighttime anxiety.[13]

Are you convinced yet? I hope so, because I can't overemphasize the importance of this piece of the depression-treatment puzzle.

As soon as Pete's brain started receiving better nutrients, he and his family were relieved to see dramatic improvements in his mood and behavior. Sensing that he was on the right path, he continued following the recommended protocol faithfully and began taking antidepressants again, which were more effective because of his supplements and diet changes. Giving his brain what it needed—through supplements and healthy eating—was an important part of the whole-person approach that turned out to be the game changer for Pete.

Depression treatment should avoid the "tried that, won't try it again" mentality. The truth is, getting your body and brain back in balance includes a lot of moving parts, and just because something didn't work the first time around doesn't mean it won't have value when tried in concert with other strategies. Giving your brain the nutrients it requires needs to happen as soon as possible, because it makes everything that follows so much more effective.

Your Personal Action Plan

Nutritional supplements provide helpful "tools" in your toolbox for overcoming depression. As you seek to fortify your body with micronutrients, start with these strategies:

1. **Evaluate your diet for possible nutrient deficiencies.** Typically, a consistent diet that includes ample fruits, vegetables, and whole grains (while avoiding processed foods)

delivers an adequate supply of fortifying nutrients. But you might be deficient in some areas without even knowing it, which could contribute to your depression. It would be worth an appointment with a nutritionist or naturopathic doctor to discuss your diet and determine if supplemental support is called for.

2. **Load up on magnesium-rich foods.** These include legumes, avocados, almonds, cashews, bananas, and fatty fish like salmon. Avoid processed foods, and learn to identify and manage your stress triggers to help preserve your magnesium status. It's also important to supplement your body's stores of magnesium. For maximum absorption and bioavailability, look for a chelated magnesium supplement.

3. **Be aware of your vitamin D intake.** How much you might need depends on the geographic region you live in, as well as the time of year, your skin type, and your level of sun exposure. To ensure that you're getting enough vitamin D, take a supplement daily.

4. **Take a good vitamin B complex to help prevent nutrient imbalances.** Because B vitamins work best in concert, don't try to pick and choose among them. Likewise, take folic acid and vitamin B_{12} together to reduce anxiety and depression.

5. **Check with your doctor before adding supplements to your diet if you are taking prescription medications.** For example, if you are on a blood thinner such as Coumadin, the additions of some vitamins and herbs to your diet can make your blood too thin.

CHAPTER 14

Reinventing Your Future

Maintain Your Momentum for the Rest of Your Life

Thus far in your journey toward healing depression for life, you've focused on the past—by facing toxic emotions and thought patterns that have kept you trapped, by owning up to old mistakes and forgiving people who have failed you in one way or another, and by examining how your own choices have helped create your experience of life.

You've also given significant thought to the present. You've considered vital issues such as current addictions, sleep habits, diet, and unhelpful behavioral patterns that have dominated your daily life. Together we've examined the various treatment options available to you today in your quest to be free of depression for good.

Now, if you've truly invested the will and the work necessary to take charge of your healing, the moment has come for you to reap the full reward. It's time to think about the *future*.

When you picked up this book and took your first steps on the road to recovery, the future probably felt like a black hole—no light, no hope of escape, no clear beginning or end. That's the nature of depression. Any attempt to see beyond present darkness becomes incredibly frightening, so you stop trying. But now that well-being is a reality for you again, and momentum is back on your side, it's time to take another look.

It's once again safe to think bigger and aim higher than you did when simply "getting by." The days, weeks, and years ahead are firmly in your control.

Don't Settle for Normal

By the time Stephanie came to me, she had attempted suicide three times in the previous two years. Depression had upended every area of her life to the point of near complete dysfunction. Just twenty-nine years old, she was a chain-smoker and drank an average of ten liters of caffeinated soda every day. She slept no more than a few hours a day and spent the other groggy twenty-one hours channel surfing between cable news programs. No frightening or ugly thing could happen in the world without Stephanie's knowledge.

After many disappointing attempts at intervention, her parents and siblings had all but given up on her. She would listen politely, concede that her life was a wreck, and then do nothing. Not surprisingly, she seemed ready to give up on herself—almost. Grasping one last time at frail hope, she agreed to our help.

The next few weeks proved one thing beyond any doubt: beneath all her troubles, Stephanie was a fighter. After a predictably rough start, she muscled her way through everything my staff and I challenged her to do. As she began to emerge from the fog of exhaustion, poor nutrition, substance abuse, and toxic thoughts and emotions, Stephanie felt better than she had in years. That sensation multiplied her motivation to succeed. And so she did. There was more work to do, but she had successfully torn out the old, crumbling foundation of her life and laid a new one, ready to start rebuilding.

And yet, just before leaving our clinic for home, Stephanie approached me with a look of panic on her face. She came to my office to talk, and the reason for her distress poured out in a confused tangle.

"I have no idea what comes next," she said, on the verge of tears. "For so long, just getting back to normal seemed impossible. Now I realize, I don't know what else to hope for!"

Stephanie expressed a common fear among people coming out of a lengthy bout with depression. It is summed up in the question *Now what?* After months or years of barely getting through the day, achieving more than that feels like an unreachable fantasy—even after the fog has lifted.

Back to the Future

I'm happy to tell you it's no fantasy! You haven't fought this hard and come this far just to plod through a mediocre life. An *extraordinary* future is now yours for the taking. You're free—not just from depression but free to succeed, to grow, to have adventures, to meet new people, to learn new things, to experience new reasons to love life. In other words, you are just like everyone else—empowered to have your life the way you want it. Here's how.

Reclaim Your Desires

It's remarkable how often people have trouble finishing the simple sentence "I want . . ." I don't mean lofty, beauty pageant answers like "world peace" or vengeful ones such as "I want my sister to suffer for her cruelty!" I'm talking about the ability to express our basic needs and desires. Somehow the process of growing up teaches most of us to think of what we want out of life as secondary to . . . well, just about everything and everyone else.

Sure, there's a time to work hard and sacrifice short-term satisfaction for our goals. But when that becomes all there is to living, problems arise. Desire is the fuel that powers achievement. Without it, there's a hard limit to what you will even try.

To test yourself for a lost connection to your desires, take out a piece of paper and write, "I want." Now make a list of all the ways you might answer the question. The only rule is you can't write something that's for someone else. Each item must reflect something you want for yourself. The desires can be practical ("I want a car that starts every time I turn the key") or more extravagant ("I want the beachside vacation I've dreamed of for years"). Don't overthink your desires—let them flow. Don't stop until you've listed at least twenty.

Now consider: Does this exercise make you uncomfortable? Do you find yourself thinking you don't deserve the things you've placed on the list? Is there a part of you that scoffs, *Yeah right, like* that's *ever going to happen*? Do you worry what others would think if you suddenly indulged yourself by pursuing something on the list? Does your memory replay for you all the bad things that happened the last time you dared to say, "I want . . ." and acted on your desire?

If you answered yes to any of these questions, then it's likely depression has stolen your desires from you—and it's time to take them back.

Begin by looking again at your list. How many of the items express things that you once loved but stopped doing for one reason or another? Drawing? Sailing? Cooking? Cross-country motorcycle riding? Writing a novel that is now half finished and gathering dust in the closet? Working at a job that gave you great satisfaction but little money?

Reclaiming your desires is really about remembering what you *love*. When you were a kid, nobody could stop you from doing cartwheels on the lawn, searching for arrowheads in the vacant lot down the street, reading comic books by the dozen, jumping off the high diving board once you learned you could—because you loved it.

Contrary to what you may believe, that kind of carefree passion is not just for kids. What a bleak world that would be! Fortunately, that's not the world as it really is.

Give yourself permission to want and reach for your desires . . . and the future will light up in front of you. Getting back in touch with your wants and wishes will empower you to dream again. With renewed knowledge of what brings you joy and rekindled optimism for the future, you can do away with limiting, sabotaging thoughts and revive an old dream that you abandoned . . . or create a big, bold, new one.

Reboot Your Imagination

Here's a startling truth: *everything* ever created by human beings— from the first stone wheel to the International Space Station orbiting the earth today—began as a vision located exclusively in someone's mind. In other words, before we create anything, we must first *see* it. Go ahead and test that claim for yourself. Try and fold a paper airplane without visualizing its finished shape first. How did that go? Draw a picture of a rose, but don't imagine how you'll shape the petals or what color you'll choose. It's not just difficult; it's impossible. We are made to imagine, and the world is made of our imaginings.

Here's the point: in the depths of depression, your imagination was hijacked and habituated to project only dull, dark, and dreary outcomes. That state of mind imagines worst-case scenarios. It projects hardship and lack everywhere it looks. And since seeing is the precursor to creating, is it any surprise that this is the vision the world reflected back to you?

To build a brighter future, begin by imagining—in vivid detail— exactly what you want it to look like. In contrast to your former habits, refuse to imagine anything that might go wrong. You get to choose what you see, after all. Do you want genuine romance in your life? Picture your dream partner as clearly as you can. Imagine yourself with this person, in love and fulfilled. Include laughter, affection, adventure—all the things you want in a relationship. Not only will your moment-to-moment experience of life improve when your thoughts are filled with hopeful images, but you can also rest assured that unseen cogs are shifting into place to bring your vision out of your head and into the world.

The practice of picturing what you want works with anything at all: a better job, a new home, improved health, closer relationships with your children, or anything else. That's because you'll set about creating what you envision. Every time. But the true power lies in making an ally out of your imagination where it really counts: *how you see yourself.* Replace the distorted self-image you created when depressed with a new one that's happy, healthy, powerful, prosperous, and free.

Legendary Renaissance artist Michelangelo understood very well the connection between seeing and creating. He once described the method behind his creative genius like this: "I saw the angel in the marble and carved until I set him free." Likewise, depression often leaves you feeling encased and trapped in stone, holding you back in every way. But your ability to fuel your imagination and foresee a bright future sets you free to flourish as the person God created you to be.

Revive Your Purpose

Many people hear the word *purpose* and think it applies only to epic, world-changing work. Not so. I define purpose as the *one unique thing* we each have to offer the world, no matter how big or small. Its absence might not make headlines, but it absolutely would be missed by those who stand to benefit from your gifts. Your personal purpose may be to pour all your energy and creativity into raising healthy children; to teach watercolor painting to residents in a retirement center; to be the most caring and conscientious insurance agent your clients have ever known; or to teach preschool in a way that endows kids with self-respect and self-confidence. The list of possibilities is infinite. Only you can know which one best describes you.

Here's the secret to finding your purpose: start by looking again at the list you made of things you have loved in your life. Chances are, what you're meant to do now is something you couldn't stop doing as a younger person but that you abandoned along the way. Or it may be the thing you still didn't dare put on the list but that tugs at your sleeve anyway.

Why is finding and following your purpose so important when revitalizing your future? Because it's what gets you out of bed on a dreary Monday morning in midwinter. Purpose is your answer to the question "Why?" Why keep a grip on my addictive impulses? Why watch what I eat? Why care about toxic emotions and their effect on my health and well-being? Why guard against old habits?

Because you have a purpose, a role to play in the lives of others. Those others may be abandoned animals at the local shelter or everyone who looks at a piece of your art and is inspired or moved. It may be cliché these days, but it's never been more true: the world needs *everyone* to fulfill their purpose—you included.

Recover Your Joy

It's safe to say that one thing you forgot through your struggle with depression is how to have *fun*. Admit it: some party-pooper part of you just rolled its eyes and mumbled that "fun" is for other people. The best you can hope for, you think, is not to be disappointed.

I know, because that's how I felt after months of having all my senses—including my sense of humor—bleached and hung out to dry by depression. It was as if the candy was stripped out of life and only a dry mouthful of cotton was left. Live like that for very long, and the words *pleasure* and *enjoyment* start to sound like a foreign language.

But it's instructive to notice that the word *enjoyment* means "the process of taking pleasure in something." *Process. Taking.* These are active words, things we purposely do and participate in. You can sit and wait for joy to strike spontaneously, and it sometimes does. But why would you want to, when it's possible to make it happen for yourself? As with so many other things we've discussed, the power of enjoyment is triggered by choice.

Start by silencing your inner critic, who pronounces judgment on every possible source of fun . . . before you even try it! A rafting excursion? Too wet, too dangerous. A salsa dance class with friends? Too embarrassing. A day at the amusement park? Too childish, too expensive, too loud, too many lines. The good news is, it's possible to displace objections like these with a determined decision to just do it. Will this test the boundaries of your comfort zone? Of course. That's what makes it fun!

Next, make room for humor and lightheartedness all through your day. Turn off the news and start a romantic comedy movie marathon or binge on old sitcom episodes or performances by stand-up comedians. Spend time around people who make you laugh and push you to lighten up. Make it your mission to laugh and smile so readily that people begin to wonder what you know that they don't.

It's up to you: sit on shore, or grab a surfboard and play.

Refuse to Retreat

Your life is a story. Like all stories, yours involves a hero (you), a journey (the battles you've fought), and a prize (lifelong wellness). In fact, that progression is found in every great story ever told, from ancient myths sung by firelight, to fairy tales, to modern blockbuster films. Embedded in all these stories is a blueprint for human progress. In other words, struggling is not failure; it's part of being human. It's how we change and grow stronger. As Joseph Campbell, the great mythologist and author of *The Hero with a Thousand Faces*, once wrote, "It is by going down into the abyss that we recover the treasures of life. Where you stumble, there lies your treasure."

That's great news. It means you need not look back on depression with regret but rather with hope that you've survived the ordeal in order to be stronger and better than ever.

But there is another universal truth about heroes you need to know as you look ahead to the rest of your life. True heroes—the ones we love most when we find them in books and movies and real-life stories—are never content to passively let events happen to them. They are the ones who, when things look darkest and all hope seems lost, refuse to give up or give in. They are tenacious beyond all reason. They stubbornly believe in what others say is impossible. They get back up again and again when knocked down.

Now that you've fought your way to the treasure of wellness on your own journey, it's important to dig in your heels and tap into the heroic determination to never, ever give it back. The future is yours. Defend it. Fight for it like the heroes you admire most in your favorite stories.

Your Personal Action Plan

There is nothing more exciting than realizing that the rest of your life can be what you choose to make it. Yes, unforeseen challenges will always be part of the fabric of life. But those need not have the final say in how you experience the world. That power belongs to you. Here are some tips for turning your dreams for the future into practical reality:

1. **Time travel.** Take out a sheet of paper and write the words, "When I was a kid, I loved to . . ." Write as many different items as you can muster. Use your imagination to recall every sensation. How did doing your favorite things look, feel,

sound, or taste? Write about the experience in vivid detail. Let yourself be back there again, enjoying life.

2. **Now, using that list, make a new one that starts with "I loved _____ because _____."** There are no wrong answers, only the need to be honest. The idea is not just to take a trip down memory lane but to revive the feeling of being free to follow your truest desires.

3. **Pick an item from your list—and do it.** For real. Did you love roller-skating? Buy a pair and head for the park. Finger painting? Yes! Playing piano? Make it happen, even if you have to hunt down a neglected piano at a church or nursing home. (If you do, it's certain you'll bless more people than just yourself.) Swimming, kite flying, bug collecting, playing basketball— you name it. Yes, you might feel silly and self-indulgent at first. Do it anyway.

4. **Now that you've started to recall how to think and act like a spontaneous child, add some new items to your list.** "Wouldn't it be fun to _____?" Don't hold back. Dream big. Pick one of these, and start making plans to do it!

5. **Create a poster board collage of found images that depict your vision of the rest of your life.** Yours might feature magazine photos of a sailboat and exotic beaches or a cabin in the mountains. You might select images that represent education, good health, financial stability, relationships, or possessions you can be proud of. Better yet, draw or paint the art yourself. Find quotes that inspire you, and weave them throughout your creation. When finished, hang your work somewhere you'll see it every day as a reminder of your decision to no longer settle for less than the best in your life.

Self-Assessment Tools

General Assessment of Your Depression Symptoms

This is a survey on our website (www.aplaceofhope.com) for clients seeking treatment at The Center: A Place of Hope. Answering these questions will provide a helpful snapshot of your current symptoms and status. (Following this survey is a way to score it.)

Are you currently experiencing . . .

Loss of enjoyment in established activities?

YES / NO

Restlessness, fatigue, or lack of motivation at work?

YES / NO

An increase in irritability or impatience?

YES / NO

A sense of being either wound up or weighed down?

YES / NO

A sense of being overburdened with life and its activities?

YES / NO

A lack of spiritual peace or well-being?

YES / NO

An unhealthy desire to control aspects of your personal behavior?

YES / NO

A fear of expressing strong emotions?

YES / NO

Constant anxiety or vague fear about the future?

YES / NO

A sense of being unappreciated by others?

YES / NO

Feelings of martyrdom?

YES / NO

A pattern of impulsive thinking or rash judgments?

YES / NO

Sexual difficulties or loss of interest in sexual activities?

YES / NO

Enjoyment in seeing others' discomfort?

YES / NO

Anger at God for how you feel?

YES / NO

A recurrent pattern of headaches, muscle aches, body pains?

YES / NO

Social isolation and distance from family or friends?

YES / NO

A sense of being trapped by the day's activities?

YES / NO

A pattern of pessimistic or critical comments and/or behaviors?

YES / NO

The belief that your best days are behind you?

YES / NO

A sense of being left out of life?

YES / NO

The desire to binge on high-calorie foods to make you feel better?

YES / NO

Apathy upon waking about how the day will turn out?

YES / NO

A preference just to do things yourself?

YES / NO

Recurring gastrointestinal difficulties?

YES / NO

A sense of being trapped inside your body?

YES / NO

Dread of family get-togethers or social gatherings?

YES / NO

The self-perception of being overweight, unattractive, unlovable?

YES / NO

A sense of being old, discarded, without value?

YES / NO

No motivation to try new activities?

YES / NO

A significant change in appetite?

YES / NO

Recurring disturbances in sleep patterns?

YES / NO

Increased agitation or inability to relax?

YES / NO

Fatigue, lethargy, or loss of energy?

YES / NO

Sadness, despondency, despair, or loneliness?

YES / NO

Inability to concentrate, focus, or make decisions?

YES / NO

Recurring thoughts of death or suicide?

YES / NO

Plans for suicide or an attempt at suicide?

YES / NO

How long have you been depressed?

The Center: A Place of Hope admissions 888-771-5166

Count up your yes responses. The following assessment will give you some indication of how you should proceed. Please note that this assessment is meant to be a guide and is not a substitution for professional consultation or treatment. It is designed to provide information to help assess whether you would benefit from professional counseling or treatment. Also note that depression is treatable, and a program at a reputable treatment center can help you regain your balance, happiness, and health.

35–38 YESES

This number of yeses indicates you are experiencing significant to extreme depression. Individuals who respond positively to this many questions frequently are diagnosed as having deep or severe depression. Depression at this level is serious, and especially if your feelings have persisted for some time, speaking with a reputable depression treatment center about a dedicated treatment program is recommended.

30–34 YESES

This number of yeses indicates you are likely experiencing significant depression, and individuals who respond positively to this many questions are often diagnosed as having depression that would benefit from treatment. Depression at this level can be serious, and especially if your feelings have persisted for some time, speaking with a reputable depression treatment center about a dedicated treatment program is recommended.

20-29 YESES

This number of yeses indicates you are likely experiencing depression and not just "feeling down" or "in a rut." Individuals who respond positively to this many questions are often diagnosed with depression. Depending on the intensity of some of the areas you noted (see the following "red/yellow" assessment for guidance), your depression may be serious. If so, or if your feelings have persisted for some time, speaking with a reputable depression treatment center about a dedicated treatment program is recommended.

15-19 YESES

This number of yeses indicates you may be experiencing depression and not just "feeling down" or "in a rut." Individuals who respond positively to this many questions are sometimes, but not always, diagnosed with depression. The diagnosis can depend on the intensity of some of the areas you noted.

If some of the questions you answered yes to are acute or severe, or if your feelings have persisted for a long time, speaking with a reputable depression treatment center about a dedicated treatment program can help you decide on whether treatment is a good option for you. You might consider an initial discussion with a professional mental health therapist or counselor.

LESS THAN 15 YESES

This number of yes answers indicates you likely are not experiencing clinical depression. Individuals who respond positively to this many questions usually are not diagnosed with depression. But the diagnosis can depend on the intensity of some of the areas you noted with an affirmative response.

The fact that you have completed the evaluation is an indication you believe you may be depressed. If some of the questions you answered yes to are acute or severe, or if your feelings have persisted for a long time, speaking with a reputable depression treatment center about a dedicated treatment program can help you decide on whether treatment is a good option for you. You might consider an initial discussion with a professional mental health therapist or counselor.

Assessment of Your Depression Severity: Are You in the "Yellow" Category or the "Red" Category?

Everyone has bad days and a case of the blues now and then. You might feel down because of a setback at work, trouble with your teenager, or an extended period of overwork that finally catches up with you and drags you down. But if you have experienced depressive symptoms and feelings continually for more than a few weeks, you very likely are enduring depression.

Still, there is a wide continuum of depression severity, from relatively mild on one end to extremely serious on the other end. How do you know where you fall on the mild-to-serious scale? With many clients, we use what we call the yellow list and the red list. The yellow list describes symptoms that signal caution and need to be monitored. The red list is composed of identified symptoms of clinical depression.

These indicators are like the stoplights at traffic intersections—they need to be carefully observed and acted upon. Yellow signals may not cause you to slam on the brakes, but they convey a message to slow down and pay attention. Red indicators should prompt immediate and intentional action.

As you work through the lists below, be aware that being in the yellow category doesn't mean you should stay there. Many people live with mild-to-moderate depression for months or years, which robs them of joy, fulfillment, and effectiveness at work and in other endeavors. I reiterate what I've said throughout this book: no one needs to live with depression, no matter how seemingly minor or commonplace. Take action to heal your depression for life.

Yellow List

O A loss of enjoyment in established activities

O Feeling restless, tired, or unmotivated at work

O An increase in irritability or impatience

O Feeling either wound up or weighed down

O Feeling overburdened with life and its activities

O A lack of spiritual peace or well-being

O A constant anxiety or vague fear about the future

O A fear of expressing strong emotions

O Finding relief by controlling aspects of your behavior, including what you eat or drink

O Feeling unappreciated by others

O Feeling a sense of martyrdom, as if you are constantly asked to do the work of others

O Exercising a pattern of impulsive thinking or rash judgments

O Feeling apathetic when you wake up in the morning about how the day will turn out

O Enjoying witnessing the discomfort of others

O Anger at God for how you feel

O A recurrent pattern of headaches, muscle aches, and/or body pains

O Feeling left out of life

O Feeling trapped during your day by what you have to do

O Experiencing recurring gastrointestinal difficulties

O Feeling like your best days are behind you and the future doesn't hold much promise

O Displaying a pattern of pessimistic or critical comments and/or behaviors

O Bingeing on high-calorie foods to feel better

O Feeling social isolation and distance from family or friends

O Feeling that it's easier to just do things yourself instead of wanting to work with others

O Feeling old, discarded, or without value

O Feeling trapped inside your body

O Dreading the thought of family get-togethers or social gatherings

O Feeling overweight, unattractive, or unlovable

O Sexual difficulties or a loss of interest in sexual activities

O Unmotivated to try new activities, contemplate new ideas, or enter into new relationships

Red List

O A significant change in appetite, resulting in either marked weight loss or weight gain

O Recurring disturbances in sleep patterns, resulting in difficulty falling and staying asleep or in sleeping too much

O Increased agitation or complete inability to relax

O Complete fatigue, overwhelming lethargy, or loss of energy

O Deep thoughts of sadness, despondency, despair, loneliness, or feelings of worthlessness

O Inability to concentrate, focus, or make decisions

O Recurring thoughts of death or suicide

O Planning or attempting suicide

Your Stress and Your Distress: Are They Feeding Each Other?

As we discussed in chapter 4, some stress in life is unavoidable and is often even helpful in concentrating our focus, motivating us to accomplish tasks, and possibly fueling changes for the better. But prolonged, high levels of stress are a prime contributor to depression. If it is not managed in a healthy, efficient way, stress will usually cause you to sink deeper and deeper into depression.

To help evaluate your current stress load, answer the following questions based on the previous six months. Track the number of "stress points" for each yes answer:

Points

1. Have you experienced the death of your spouse? 20
2. Have you divorced or separated from your husband or wife? 15
3. Has a close relative died (other than your spouse)? 13
4. Have you been hospitalized? 11
5. Have you married or reconciled with your partner after separation? 10
6. Have you found out you were soon to become a parent? 9
7. Has there been a change in the health of a close family member (good or bad)? 9
8. Have you lost a job or retired? 9
9. Are you having sexual difficulties? 8
10. Has a new member been born or married into your family? 8
11. Has a close friend died? 8
12. Have your finances become better or worse? 8
13. Have you changed your job? 8
14. Have any children moved out of the home, or started or finished school? 6
15. Is trouble with in-laws causing trouble in your family? 6

16. Is there anyone at home or work you dislike strongly? 6
17. Do you frequently have premenstrual tension? 6
18. Have you had important personal success (such as a job promotion)? 6
19. Have you had "jet lag" (travel fatigue) at least twice? 6
20. Have you had a major domestic upheaval, such as a move or remodeling of your home? 5
21. Have you had problems at work that may be putting your job at risk? 5
22. Have you taken on a large debt or mortgage? 3
23. Have you had a minor brush with the law (i.e., a traffic violation)? 2

Assessment: Obviously, the higher your score, the more stressful your life is. As a guideline, a score of thirty suggests you are not likely at a stress level that is greatly affecting your depression. Trouble increases as you move up the point scale. If your score is sixty or more, your life is extremely stressful, which is almost certainly contributing to your depression. In this case, you need to manage your current stress purposefully and, insofar as you're able, make decisions and lifestyle choices that avoid adding more stress in the future.

Leave No Stone Unturned

Further Treatment Options Worth Exploring

In the preceding chapters we examined many of the pillars of good mental health. When you are committed to getting plenty of nutrients, exercise, and sleep; when you free yourself from toxins, addictions, and grudges; when you embrace healthy spiritual practices; and when you take action to manage and reduce stress in your life, you are well on your way to better health all the way around. Your mental health will be improved, and your physical health will be too.

As foundational as these actions are, they are not exhaustive. There is a wide array of treatment options you can explore in your pursuit of wholeness and healing. In my whole-person approach to dealing with depression, I encourage people to try anything that is safe and sane. The treatments described below are options you may want to consider.

Acupuncture

This is a technique in which very thin needles are inserted through the skin to stimulate strategic points on the body. According to traditional medicine in China, where acupuncture originated, there are some two thousand acupuncture points on the body that can be stimulated to balance the flow of energy throughout the body. Western medicine more typically regards acupuncture as a way to strategically stimulate nerves and muscles, which increases blood flow and activates the body to produce endorphins and opioids, which are natural painkillers.

Acupuncture has been used to relieve dental pain, headaches, neck and back pain, knee pain, high and low blood pressure, and morning sickness. Increasingly, it is being used to relieve symptoms of depression as well.

While studies examining acupuncture's impact on depression are limited, they are promising. For example, in a randomized controlled study, 755 depressed patients were divided into groups that received acupuncture, counseling, or neither. After three months, acupuncture and counseling both proved effective at significantly reducing depression. Follow-up testing a year later showed similar results.

According to Professor Hugh MacPherson, who helped conceive and design the study, "In the largest study of its kind, we have now provided a solid evidence base to show that not only can acupuncture and counseling bring patients out of an episode of depression, but it can keep the condition at bay for up to a year on average."

He adds that their research "provides a significant step forward in treating chronic pain and managing depression, because patients and health professionals can now make decisions on acupuncture with more confidence. Not only is it more cost effective, but it reduces pain levels and improves mood levels, which could reduce overreliance on drugs that can sometimes result in unwanted side effects."[1]

Aromatherapy

This treatment approach uses fragrant essential oils derived from plants. When inhaled or applied to the skin, these oils can have a positive effect on physical, emotional, or mental well-being. Some of the more common reasons people turn to aromatherapy include managing pain, reducing stress, relieving symptoms of depression, improving concentration and clarity, relieving muscle soreness, and improving respiratory health.

While aromatherapy is gaining popularity in general, does it really work? Particularly with regard to the impact of aromatherapy on depression, what have various studies revealed?

According to a study conducted at Ruhr University in Bochum, Germany, brain scans of mice exposed to the scent of jasmine showed an increase in the calming neurotransmitter GABA. Some aromatherapy advocates "suggest that essential oils may affect a number of biological factors, including heart rate, stress levels, blood pressure, breathing, and immune function."[2]

To determine what other researchers are saying on this matter, a systematic review identified twelve randomized controlled trials dealing specifically with aromatherapy and depression. Five of the studies looked at inhalation therapy, while seven studies evaluated the effectiveness of aromatherapy when used in combination with massage therapy. According to these studies, the aromatherapy/massage combination showed to have more benefits than inhalation therapy alone.[3]

Researchers have identified a number of essential oils that appear to have the most potential for alleviating depression symptoms. These include:

- bergamot and sweet orange: linked to reducing anxiety and stress
- bergamot, lavender, and frankincense: showed a positive impact on pain and depression among people with cancer
- lavender: can improve sleep in general and also decrease anxiety, stress, and depression
- rosemary, rose, and wild ginger: showed benefits for people with depression

- ylang ylang: can have a positive impact on heart rate, blood pressure, and breathing
- grapefruit: can alleviate mental exhaustion and fatigue and has been identified alongside other citrus oils in a 1995 study as potentially being "more effective than antidepressants"[4]

Aromatherapy may seem like a simple intervention, and it is. When using essential oils topically, never apply full-strength oils directly to your skin. Instead, add a few drops to an ounce of almond, olive, or coconut oil. If you prefer to inhale the oils, pass an open bottle beneath your nose, or put a few drops in an electric diffuser or a bowl of steaming hot water.

Ketamine/Esketamine

Ketamine was developed in the 1960s as an anesthetic for humans and animals. In addition to dulling pain, it's known for creating the sensation of being detached from your own body.

It is also used to treat severe depression, suicidal thoughts, and post-traumatic stress disorder (PTSD).

How does the drug work? Research is still relatively new, and studies are examining the exact nature of the drug's interaction with the human body. But it appears that—unlike antidepressants, which adjust the balance of brain chemicals like dopamine and serotonin—ketamine generates the creation of new synapses and improves communication between neurons.

What makes ketamine particularly beneficial is how quickly it works to improve mood. In 2006, researchers at the National Institutes of Health discovered that ketamine could relieve severe depression and suicidal thoughts in a matter of hours. "There is a desperate need for a better treatment for those who are suicidal," explains Jennifer Vande Voort, a psychiatrist at Mayo Clinic in

Rochester, Minnesota. "The fact that it's rapid-acting . . . that type of treatment can save lives."[5]

In fact, the results have been so dramatic that Janssen Pharmaceutical Companies of Johnson & Johnson are currently completing clinical trials of esketamine, a nasal-spray form of ketamine. Forty-nine patients completed the four-week clinical trials and saw a significant decrease in depression symptoms in just four hours.[6]

A possible downside of ketamine and esketamine is that the drug has a history of abuse as a club party drug, popular in the seventies and eighties. Does the drug have the potential of creating a population of addicts, much like prescription opioids have done?

The jury is still out, but it's worth paying attention to the progress made with this drug in the near future. Further research will clarify the potential dangers and benefits of this treatment option.

Light Therapy

Seasonal affective disorder (SAD) is a form of depression related to the change of seasons and typically occurs the same time each year, usually beginning in the fall and continuing through the winter months. "Winter depression" symptoms can include sleeping more, eating more high-carb foods, gaining weight, and feeling fatigued.

Less common is a spring or summer onset of SAD. The symptoms of "summer depression" are inverse to those of winter depression and can include insomnia, loss of appetite, weight loss, and agitation.

Both winter and summer depression are marked by other symptoms of major depression, including feeling depressed most of the time, feeling hopeless or worthless, losing interest in activities previously considered enjoyable, having difficulty concentrating, or experiencing recurring thoughts of death or suicide.

Light therapy is used to treat SAD as well as other types of depression. The treatment is relatively simple: patients sit in front of a light box—which emits a full-spectrum bright light—typically for thirty minutes a day. The recommended duration of treatment is generally to continue using the light box well into spring.

Does it work? The answer seems to be a resounding *yes*. Our team sees exceptional results from light therapy with clients at The Center: A Place of Hope. What's more, studies show that seven out of ten patients experience relief from SAD symptoms within a few weeks of beginning treatment. We have long known that getting enough sunlight is important for staving off depression. As it turns out, artificial light helps too, affecting parts of the brain associated with mood and sleep.

Massage Therapy

Who doesn't love a massage? Most of us do, and for good reason. The health benefits of massages are varied and well documented.

For starters, studies have shown that massages reduce cortisol—the stress hormone—by 31 percent, while at the same time increasing mood-boosting hormones like dopamine and serotonin by as much as a third.

The mood-boosting benefits of massage are important, particularly for people suffering from depression. Massage also lowers stress and can improve sleep, which, as we've seen in earlier chapters, can have a dramatic impact on the severity of symptoms of depression.

Why does massage make such a difference? According to psychologist Tiffany Field, director of the University of Miami Touch Research Institute, massage stimulates pressure receptors under the skin, which in turn stimulates the vagus nerve. The word *vagus* means "wandering," and this nerve does indeed wander all through the body, reaching the brain, gut, heart, liver, pancreas, gallbladder, kidney, spleen, and esophagus.

The benefits of stimulating this nerve are many, but of particular interest to people with depression is the fact that stimulating this nerve has positive impacts on mood. In fact, there is an intervention used for severe depression called vagus nerve stimulation (VNS), which utilizes a device implanted beneath the skin to deliver electrical pulses to this nerve.[7] Massages are an obviously less invasive and less costly way to stimulate this important nerve. According to Dr. Field, many forms of exercise can also stimulate our pressure receptors, providing benefits similar to those of getting a massage.

Transcranial Magnetic Stimulation (TMS)

This therapeutic technique does just what the name implies: it uses magnetic fields to stimulate parts of the brain associated with depression. This is a noninvasive treatment in which an electromagnet coil is placed on the scalp near the front of the head. A magnetic pulse stimulates nerve cells related to mood and can increase activity in parts of the brain that are typically underactive for people with depression.[8] Sessions last about half an hour and are delivered five days a week for up to six weeks.

This treatment is often tried when other treatments—such as antidepressants—have not resulted in improvement. Among those who receive this treatment, more than half experience improvements, and a third report that their symptoms are eliminated completely. And while relapse can occur, a study reported in the *Journal of Affective Disorders* determined that patients who received maintenance TMS treatments were significantly less likely to relapse than those who did not receive additional treatments.[9] Another study out of Rush University Medical Center in Chicago showed a low relapse rate among the 301 patients who took part in the study, and according to lead researcher Philip Janicak, MD, the results "further support TMS as a viable treatment option for patients with major depression who have not responded to conventional antidepressant medications."[10]

TMS has shown such promising results for people with depression that studies are currently under way on the use of TMS with patients with Alzheimer's,[11] as well as ADHD, strokes, and PTSD.[12]

While most research evaluates the impact of stand-alone TMS, in the real world this treatment option is often combined with talk therapy and other treatments. At The Center, we have found that TMS works best when combined with our whole-person approach.

Don't Give Up

One of the reasons to familiarize yourself with the many treatments for depression is because the mental health field is always changing and growing. You have access today to interventions that did not exist five years ago; five years from now you will have access to even more.

Wherever you are in your pursuit of better mental and emotional health, there is always room for growth and improvement. It's true that among the dozens of depression-related treatments, some are "out there"—unproven and unsubstantiated by solid research. Many others, however, are based on scientific study and are worth exploring. Use commonsense precautions, conduct your own research, and if in doubt, discuss your intended treatment option with your physician.

The important message here is to continue learning and trying new things. One of the hallmarks of depression is losing interest in many things, including personal development. And this is exactly why you must make ongoing efforts to explore and embrace new ideas and behaviors, particularly when they have the potential for creating lasting, positive changes in your life.

Whole Health Matters

Seven Ways to Take Responsibility for Your Wellness—and Relieve Your Depression

If there's anything I've tried to drive home in the pages of this book, it's that depression must be evaluated—and addressed—in the context of the whole person. In the preceding chapters, we've addressed many physical conditions—from sleep apnea and stress to malnutrition and heart disease—that are linked to depression.

But the list doesn't stop there. Additional physical conditions that can contribute to depression include hypothyroidism or thyroid deficiency, menopause, low testosterone in men, diabetes, childbirth, and even puberty.

And if a condition you are addressing with medication isn't linked to depression, the medication you are taking could be. There are literally hundreds of medications on the market today with depression as a possible side effect. Oral contraceptives, for example, can hinder the production of serotonin, affecting mood and sleep. Certain acid reflux interventions (like Prilosec), blood pressure medications, anxiety medications, and painkillers have the potential of causing depression. In fact, based on a study of 26,192 adults published by the *Journal of the American Medical Association*, researchers concluded that an estimated one out of three adults in America is taking medications for which potential side effects include depression and/or suicidal thoughts.[1]

So where does this leave you? What steps can you take to make sure past (or current) health issues are not contributing to feelings of depression?

Here are seven principles you can follow to help you take care of, well, *you*.

1. Don't Ignore What Ails You

Many people have the attitude of "ignore it and hope it goes away." In this case, ignorance is not bliss. Most health concerns are like cavities in your teeth: they're not going to get better; in fact, they will likely get worse without treatment from a skilled professional. When it comes to your physical, mental, and emotional health, denial is not your friend.

2. Stop Procrastinating

Sometimes we have every intention of getting to a doctor or addressing an issue. We're not in denial—we know there is something going on that needs to be solved. Maybe we even understand that the matter is serious. It's on our to-do list . . . it just never gets done.

The reasons we procrastinate are many and can vary by person. It's possible that some people procrastinate due to poor time management, but that's unlikely. The truth is that we are very good at making time for things we consider important (or even just enjoyable—for example, how many hours have you spent on social media this week?).

Procrastination is more often related to negative feelings (such as fear) or perceived needs (such as the need to be in control) that we have attached to the task at hand.

Even shame can play a role in procrastination. This was the case for one of my clients, who put off seeing a doctor for acid reflux for years because she felt ashamed that her eating habits and excess weight were at the root of her condition.

The need to act passive aggressively toward someone who is pestering you to get help can also trigger procrastination. The more someone nudges you, the more you resist.

In addition to creating an environment in which small health problems can potentially bloom into bigger problems, studies show that procrastination itself is bad for you, increasing stress and anxiety and decreasing the quality of your sleep,[2] which impacts things like weight gain, the immune system, and more.

Figuring out what is fueling your procrastination can be helpful, but it's not necessary. Procrastination can be solved—and solved quickly—by simply doing the thing you've been putting off.

3. Stay Current on Your Particular Condition

In our modern era, new research is conducted on nearly all diseases and conditions each year. With a simple online search, you can stay up to date on the latest discoveries and treatment options. You can also join online groups or subscribe to e-newsletters related to your unique health issues.

And if your doctor recommends periodic evaluations or check-ins, don't neglect appointments of this nature because you are currently feeling good or symptom free. The best way to *stay* that way is to maintain your care. I can't tell you how many people I see who follow the protocols I give them long enough to experience some improvement and then, because they are feeling better, stop the behaviors that are working for them. As a caregiver, it's frustrating to watch people who have experienced some measure of success sabotage their physical, mental, and emotional health because they are no longer struggling, only to reencounter problems because they abandoned the tools that led to their success.

4. Assess Your Medications

Because so many drugs can contribute to depression, if you are experiencing symptoms of depression, have a health care professional assess the medications you are taking to see if any might be adding to your struggle. Ask if dosages of suspect drugs can be adjusted, eliminated, or replaced with a different drug or treatment.

5. Be Your Own Advocate

In the current health care environment, you can't count on anyone but yourself to safeguard your health. Even if you are fortunate enough to have history with a physician who has tracked and treated your health concerns, it is still up to you to take care of yourself.

One of the ways you can do this is by being prepared when you go to your appointments. Write down any issues you want to discuss with your caregiver ahead of time. It's extremely frustrating to wait weeks for an appointment, then realize when you get home that you forgot to bring up something important.

Another way to take care of yourself is to be willing to explore new treatment options, schedule appointments with specialists, and pursue nontraditional healing pathways. Casting your net wide to compile a team of skilled professionals who care about your health takes time and effort, but you will reap the rewards in a longer and healthier life.

Finally, understanding your insurance and health care options goes a long way. Choosing the right doctors and the right treatments is easier when you understand what is available to you.

6. Keep Good Records of Your Health History

Your medical history is important and may inform future treatments and techniques to bring healing. It can shed light on current struggles

and provide invaluable information to current health care professionals. Keep good records of past ailments, who has treated you, and any
medications you have taken.

7. Enlist an Accountability Partner

The power of accountability can't be denied. According to a study
conducted by the American Society of Training and Development,
when you make a goal-related commitment to a friend or coach,
the likelihood of completing that goal goes up to 65 percent. And
if you make a specific appointment with your accountability partner
related to your progress or results, your likelihood of success goes up
to 95 percent.[3]

When it comes to taking care of your health, how much accountability you want or need will depend on your goals and situation.
After all, it may not make sense to have a formal accountability
arrangement or daily check-in with someone. Then again, it might,
particularly if there is a new daily or weekly behavior you are striving
to embrace.

An accountability partner can ask you questions such as these: Are
you keeping up with your exercise goals? Did you take your vitamin
D today? Did you meet your water-intake goal for today? Are you
making the health care appointments you said you needed to make?
Did you get in touch with that doctor about your depression symptoms like you promised you would?

Giving someone permission to ask about the health goals we set
for ourselves makes sense. Accountability partners don't "make" us do
anything. They don't even tell us what to do. They check in and ask
us how we are succeeding at the things we say we want to do. And
sometimes that can make all the difference in the world.

When it comes to your health, you're in charge. No one knows what you are experiencing as well as you do, and you are also the person with the greatest access to the decisions and behaviors that can have the most significant impact on how you feel. No one can do this for you. By accepting responsibility for your wellness, you will be on your way to optimizing your physical health, and your mental and emotional health too. For more than thirty years, my team and I have seen the whole-person approach work time and time again . . . largely because people have taken the responsibility and summoned the courage to ensure their healing and wellness.

Recommended Resources

Books on Nutrition and Depression

21 Days to Eating Better: A Proven Plan for Beginning New Habits by Gregory L. Jantz (Zondervan, 1998).

The Body God Designed: How to Love the Body You've Got While You Get the Body You Want by Gregory L. Jantz (Strang, 2007).

Breakthrough Depression Solution: Mastering Your Mood with Nutrition, Diet and Supplementation by James M. Greenblatt (Sunrise River Press, 2016).

Happy Gut: The Cleansing Program to Help You Lose Weight, Gain Energy, and Eliminate Pain by Vincent Pedre (HarperCollins, 2015).

The Microbiome Diet: The Scientifically Proven Way to Restore Your Gut Health and Achieve Permanent Weight Loss by Raphael Kellman (Da Capo Lifelong Books, 2014).

The Microbiome Solution: A Radical New Way to Heal Your Body from the Inside Out by Robynne Chutkan (Avery Books, 2015).

The Psychobiotic Revolution: Mood, Food, and the New Science of the Gut-Brain Connection by Scott C. Anderson with John F. Cryan and Ted Dinan (National Geographic, 2017).

The UltraMind Solution: The Simple Way to Defeat Depression, Overcome Anxiety, and Sharpen Your Mind by Mark Hyman (Scribner, 2009).

Books on Exercise and Depression

8 Keys to Mental Health through Exercise by Christina G. Hibbert (W. W. Norton, 2016).

Exercise for Mood and Anxiety: Proven Strategies for Overcoming Depression and Enhancing Well-Being by Michael W. Otto and Jasper A. J. Smits (Oxford University Press, 2011).

Spark: The Revolutionary New Science of Exercise and the Brain by John J. Ratey with Eric Hagerman (Little, Brown, 2013).

Books on Emotional Health and Depression

Anatomy of an Epidemic: Magic Bullets, Psychiatric Drugs, and the Astonishing Rise of Mental Illness in America by Robert Whitaker (Broadway Books, 2015).

Controlling Your Anger before It Controls You: A Guide for Women by Gregory L. Jantz with Ann McMurray (Revell, 2013).

Depression Sourcebook, edited by Keith Jones, Health Reference Series (Omnigraphics, 2017).

Happy for the Rest of Your Life: Four Steps to Contentment, Hope, and Joy—and Three Keys to Staying There by Gregory L. Jantz with Ann McMurray (Siloam, 2009).

Healing the Scars of Childhood Abuse: Moving beyond the Past into a Healthy Future by Gregory L. Jantz with Ann McMurray (Revell, 2017).

How to De-Stress Your Life by Gregory L. Jantz (Revell, 1998).

Overcoming Anxiety, Worry, and Fear by Gregory L. Jantz (Revell, 2011).

Self-Coaching: The Powerful Program to Beat Anxiety and Depression by Joseph J. Luciani (John Wiley & Sons, Inc., 2007).

Uncovering Happiness: Overcoming Depression with Mindfulness and Self-Compassion by Elisha Goldstein (Atria Books, 2015).

The Upward Spiral: Using Neuroscience to Reverse the Course of Depression, One Small Change at a Time by Alex Korb (New Harbinger Publications, 2015).

Books on Spirituality and Depression

The Blessing: Giving the Gift of Unconditional Love and Acceptance by John Trent and Gary Smalley (Thomas Nelson, 2004).

How to Forgive . . . When You Don't Feel Like It by June Hunt (Harvest House, 2015).

The Inner Voice of Love: A Journey through Anguish to Freedom by Henri J. M. Nouwen (Image Books, 1999).

Jesus Wept: When Faith and Depression Meet by Barbara C. Crafton (Jossey-Bass, 2009).

Unshakable Hope: Building Our Lives on the Promises of God by Max Lucado (Thomas Nelson, 2018).

Books on Technology and Depression

12 Ways Your Phone Is Changing You by Tony Reinke (Crossway, 2017).

Alone Together: Why We Expect More from Technology and Less from Each Other by Sherry Turkle (Basic Books, 2011).

#Hooked: The Pitfalls of Media, Technology, and Social Networking by Gregory L. Jantz with Ann McMurray (Siloam, 2012).

iDisorder: Understanding Our Obsession with Technology and Overcoming Its Hold on Us by Larry Rosen (Palgrave Macmillan, 2012).

iGen: Why Today's Super-Connected Kids Are Growing Up Less Rebellious, More Tolerant, Less Happy—and Completely Unprepared for Adulthood by Jean M. Twenge (Atria Books, 2017).

Irresistible: The Rise of Addictive Technology and the Business of Keeping Us Hooked by Adam Alter (Penguin Books, 2018).

Rewired: Understanding the iGeneration and the Way They Learn by Larry D. Rosen with L. Mark Carrier and Nancy A. Cheever (Palgrave Macmillan, 2010).

Books on Addiction and Depression

Don't Call It Love: Breaking the Cycle of Relationship Dependency by Gregory L. Jantz and Tim Clinton with Ann McMurray (Revell, 2015).

Food Junkies: The Truth about Food Addiction by Vera Tarman with Philip Werdell (Dundurn Press, 2014).

Healing the Scars of Addiction: Reclaiming Your Life and Moving into a Healthy Future by Gregory L. Jantz with Ann McMurray (Revell, 2018).

Organizations Offering Help for Depression and Mental Health

American Association of Christian Counselors. www.aacc.net. AACC assists Christian counselors, licensed professionals, pastors, and lay church members.

American Psychological Association. www.apa.org. The largest association of psychologists in the world, the APA offers access to the latest information on depression and related conditions like ADHD, eating disorders, and suicide.

Anxiety and Depression Association of America. www.adaa .org. This organization provides detailed facts about various conditions, including depression and its symptoms.

Brain and Behavior Research Foundation. www.bbrfoundation .org. This site provides information about depression, anxiety, and other related conditions. The foundation provides support for research into depression and related conditions.

Depression and Bipolar Support Alliance. www.dbsalliance .org. This is a self-help organization for patients and family members, providing significant information on depression as well as anxiety and bipolar disorder.

Mental Health America. www.mentalhealthamerica.net. This is one of the foremost nonprofit organizations in the mental health field, providing up-to-date news and information.

National Alliance on Mental Illness. www.nami.org. This organization provides education and support pertaining to a wide variety of mental health conditions.

National Institute of Mental Health. www.nimh.nih.gov. As the country's largest organization focusing on mental health conditions, NIMH publishes detailed information about the latest findings on depression, anxiety, ADHD, OCD, and related conditions.

Notes

INTRODUCTION: HELP IS ON THE WAY

1. A. H. Weinberger et al., "Trends in Depression Prevalence in the USA from 2005 to 2015: Widening Disparities in Vulnerable Groups," *Psychological Medicine* 48, no. 8 (June 2018): 1308–15, https://www.cambridge.org/core/journals/psychological -medicine/article/trends-in-depression-prevalence-in-the-usa-from-2005-to-2015 -widening-disparities-in-vulnerable-groups/8A2904A85BB1F4436102DB78 E3854E35. See also Maggie Fox, "Major Depression on the Rise among Everyone, New Data Shows," NBC News, May 10, 2018, https://www.nbcnews.com/health /health-news/major-depression-rise-among-everyone-new-data-shows-n873146.

2. Kashmira Gander, "Depression Is a Potential Side Effect of Over 200 Common Prescription Drugs, Scientists Warn," *Newsweek*, June 13, 2018, https://www .newsweek.com/depression-potential-side-effect-over-200-common-prescription -drugs-scientists-974358.

CHAPTER 1: FINDING A NEW PATH FORWARD

1. World Health Organization, "'Depression: Let's Talk' Says WHO, as Depression Tops List of Causes of Ill Health," news release, March 30, 2017, http://www.who .int/news-room/detail/30-03-2017--depression-let-s-talk-says-who-as-depression -tops-list-of-causes-of-ill-health.

2. "Major Depression," National Institute of Mental Health, updated November 2017, https://www.nimh.nih.gov/health/statistics/major-depression.shtml.

3. A summary of research findings can be accessed at Seth J. Gillihan, "What Is the Best Way to Treat Depression?" *Psychology Today*, May 30, 2017, https://www.psychology today.com/us/blog/think-act-be/201705/what-is-the-best-way-treat-depression. Also see P. Cuijpers et al., "A Meta-analysis of Cognitive-Behavioural Therapy for Adult Depression, Alone and In Comparison with Other Treatments," *Canadian Journal of Psychiatry* 58, no. 7 (July 2013): 376–85, https://www.ncbi.nlm.nih.gov/pubmed /23870719; S. M. de Maat et al., "Relative Efficacy of Psychotherapy and Combined

Therapy in the Treatment of Depression: A Meta-analysis," *European Psychiatry* 22, no. 1 (January 2007): 1–8, https://www.ncbi.nlm.nih.gov/pubmed/17194571.

4. "Depression Basics," National Institute of Mental Health, revised 2016, https://www.nimh.nih.gov/health/publications/depression/index.shtml.

CHAPTER 2: SOUND ASLEEP

1. "1 in 3 Adults Don't Get Enough Sleep," CDC Newsroom, CDC, last modified February 16, 2016, https://www.cdc.gov/media/releases/2016/p0215-enough-sleep .html. See also "Data and Statistics: Short Sleep Duration among US Adults," Sleep and Sleep Disorders, CDC, last modified May 2, 2017, https://www.cdc.gov/sleep /data_statistics.html.

2. National Sleep Foundation, *2011 Sleep in America® Poll: Communications Technology in the Bedroom* (Washington, DC: The Foundation, March 7, 2011), https://sleep foundation.org/sites/default/files/sleepinamericapoll/SIAP_2011_Summary_of _Findings.pdf.

3. Ibid.

4. Rachael Rettner, "Nighttime Gadget Use Interferes with Young Adults' Health," Live Science, March 10, 2011, https://www.livescience.com/35536-technology-sleep -adolescents.html.

5. Neralie Cain and Michael Gradisar, "Electronic Media Use and Sleep in School-Aged Children and Adolescents: A Review," *Sleep Medicine* 11, no. 8 (September 2010): 735–42, https://doi.org/10.1016/j.sleep.2010.02.006.

6. "Nearly 7 in 10 Americans Are on Prescription Drugs," *ScienceDaily*, June 19, 2013, https://www.sciencedaily.com/releases/2013/06/130619132352.htm.

7. Most of the dementing illnesses—Alzheimer's disease, vascular dementia, Lewy body dementia, and Parkinson's disease—cause "irreversible damage" to the parts of the brain that regulate sleep. Sleep disturbances are virtually unavoidable and, if not addressed, exacerbate problems such as daytime sleepiness, confusion, and agitated behavior experienced by people with dementia, as well as the challenges experienced by caregivers. See Jana R. Cooke and Sonia Ancoli-Israel, "Normal and Abnormal Sleep in the Elderly," *Handbook of Clinical Neurology* 98 (2011): 653–65, https:// www.ncbi.nlm.nih.gov/pmc/articles/PMC3142094/.

8. Harvard Health Publishing, "Insomnia in Later Life," *Harvard Mental Health Letter*, December 2006, https://www.health.harvard.edu/newsletter_article/Insomnia_in _later_life.

9. David Nutt, Sue Wilson, and Louise Paterson, "Sleep Disorders as Core Symptoms of Depression," *Dialogues in Clinical Neuroscience* 10, no. 3 (September 2008): 329–36, https://www.ncbi.nlm.nih.gov/pmc/articles/PMC3181883/.

10. Mary O'Brien, *The Healing Power of Sleep* (Concord, CA: Biomed Books, 2009), 16–17.

11. Cass Edwards et al., "Depressive Symptoms before and after Treatment of Obstructive Sleep Apnea in Men and Women," *Journal of Clinical Sleep Medicine* 11, no. 9 (September 15, 2015): 1029–38, https://www.ncbi.nlm.nih.gov/pmc/articles /PMC4543247/.

12. O'Brien, *Healing Power of Sleep*, 47.

13. Rachel Manber et al., "Cognitive Behavioral Therapy for Insomnia Enhances Depression Outcome in Patients with Comorbid Major Depressive Disorder and Insomnia," *Sleep* 31, no. 4 (April 1, 2008): 489–95, https://www.ncbi.nlm.nih.gov /pmc/articles/PMC2279754/.

14. Benedict Carey, "Sleep Therapy Seen as an Aid for Depression," *New York Times*, November 18, 2013, https://www.nytimes.com/2013/11/19/health/treating -insomnia-to-heal-depression.html.

15. Michael Scullin, quoted at Amanda MacMillan, "Do This One Simple Thing to Fall Asleep Faster," *Time*, January 12, 2018, http://time.com/5097840/how-to -fall-asleep-faster/.

CHAPTER 3: YOUR DEVICES, YOUR DEPRESSION

1. Liu yi Lin et al., "Association between Social Media Use and Depression among U.S. Young Adults," *Depression and Anxiety* 33, no. 4 (April 2016): 323–31, https://www .ncbi.nlm.nih.gov/pmc/articles/PMC4853817/.

2. Phoebe Weston, "Are Teenagers Replacing Drugs and Alcohol with Technology? Experts Describe Smartphones as 'Digital Heroin' for Millennials," *Daily Mail*, March 14, 2017, http://www.dailymail.co.uk/sciencetech/article-4313278/Are -teenagers-replacing-drugs-alcohol-TECHNOLOGY.html.

3. Anna Fifield, "In South Korea, a Rehab Camp for Internet-Addicted Teenagers," *Washington Post*, January 24, 2016, https://www.washingtonpost.com/world/asia _pacific/in-south-korea-a-rehab-camp-for-internet-addicted-teenagers/2016/01 /24/9c143ab4-b965-11e5-85cd-5ad59bc19432_story.html?noredirect=on&utm _term=.e548f3336df3.

4. Cecilia Cheng and Angel Yee-lam Li, "Internet Addiction Prevalence and Quality of (Real) Life: A Meta-analysis of 31 Nations across Seven World Regions," *Cyberpsychology, Behavior, and Social Networking* 17, no. 12 (December 9, 2014), https://www.liebertpub.com/doi/full/10.1089/cyber.2014.0317.

5. Maeve Duggan, "Online Harassment 2017," Pew Research Center, July 11, 2017, http://www.pewinternet.org/2017/07/11/online-harassment-2017/.

6. Michael Gurian, *The Wonder of Boys: What Parents, Mentors and Educators Can Do to Shape Boys into Exceptional Men* (New York: Penguin, 2006), 215.

7. Lynette L. Craft and Frank M. Perna, "The Benefits of Exercise for the Clinically Depressed," *Primary Care Companion to the Journal of Clinical Psychiatry* 6, no. 3 (2004): 104–11, https://www.ncbi.nlm.nih.gov/pmc/articles/PMC474733/.

8. Linda Stone, "Continuous Partial Attention," *Linda Stone* (blog), accessed December 7, 2018, https://lindastone.net/qa/continuous-partial-attention/.

CHAPTER 4: STRESSED AND DEPRESSED

1. George M. Slavich and Michael R. Irwin, "From Stress to Inflammation and Major Depressive Disorder: A Social Signal Transduction Theory of Depression," *Psychological Bulletin* 140, no. 3 (May 2014): 774–815, https://www.ncbi.nlm.nih .gov/pmc/articles/PMC4006295/.

2. Janice K. Kiecolt-Glaser, Heather M. Derry, and Christopher P. Fagundes, "Inflammation: Depression Fans the Flames and Feasts on the Heat," *American*

Journal of Psychiatry 172, no. 11 (November 1, 2015): 1075–91, https://ajp
.psychiatryonline.org/doi/10.1176/appi.ajp.2015.15020152.

3. Norman B. Anderson, quoted at R. A. Clay, "Stressed in America," *Monitor on
Psychology* 42, no. 1 (January 2011): 60, https://www.apa.org/monitor/2011/01
/stressed-america.aspx.

4. American Psychological Association, "2015 Stress in America," news release, accessed
March 2, 2019, http://www.apa.org/news/press/releases/stress/2015/snapshot.aspx.

5. Bernard Marr, "Why Too Much Data Is Stressing Us Out," *Forbes*, November 25,
2015, https://www.forbes.com/sites/bernardmarr/2015/11/25/why-too-much-data
-is-stressing-us-out/#5325947f7630.

6. "Jettisoning Work Email Reduces Stress," UCI News, May 3, 2012, https://news.uci
.edu/2012/05/03/jettisoning-work-email-reduces-stress/.

7. American Psychological Association, "2015 Stress in America."

8. Joseph Ferrari and Timothy Pychyl, quoted at Hara Estroff Marano, "Why We
Procrastinate," *Psychology Today*, July 1, 2005, https://www.psychologytoday.com/us
/articles/200507/why-we-procrastinate.

9. Therese J. Borchard, "Spirituality and Prayer Relieve Stress," Psych Central, updated
July 8, 2018, https://psychcentral.com/blog/spirituality-and-prayer-relieve-stress/.

10. Sammi R. Chekroud et al., "Association between Physical Exercise and Mental
Health in 1.2 Million Individuals in the USA between 2011 and 2015: A Cross-
Sectional Study," *Lancet Psychiatry* 5, no. 9 (August 8, 2018): 739–46, https://www
.thelancet.com/journals/lanpsy/article/PIIS2215-0366(18)30227-X/fulltext.

CHAPTER 5: A HARD LOOK AT HARD ISSUES

1. Substance Abuse and Mental Health Services Administration, *Behavioral Health
Trends in the United States: Results from the 2014 National Survey on Drug Use and
Health*, September 2015, https://www.samhsa.gov/data/sites/default/files/NSDUH
-FRR1-2014/NSDUH-FRR1-2014.pdf.

2. Justin D. Wareham and Marc N. Potenza, "Pathological Gambling and Substance Use
Disorders," *American Journal of Drug and Alcohol Abuse* 36, no. 5 (September 2010):
242–47, https://www.ncbi.nlm.nih.gov/pmc/articles/PMC3671380/.

3. National Council on Problem Gambling, *Problem and Pathological Gambling in
America: The National Picture* (1997), 14–15.

4. Substance Abuse and Mental Health Services Administration, "General Facts and
Recommendations" regarding *Facing Addiction in America: The Surgeon General's
Report on Alcohol, Drugs, and Health*, 2016, https://addiction.surgeongeneral.gov
/sites/default/files/fact-sheet-general.pdf.

5. Linda R. Gowing et al., "Global Statistics on Addictive Behaviours: 2014 Status
Report," *Addiction* 110, no. 6 (June 2015): 904–19, https://www.ncbi.nlm.nih.gov
/pubmed/25963869.

6. Christopher Ingraham, "One in Eight American Adults Is an Alcoholic, Study Says,"
Washington Post, August 11, 2017, https://www.washingtonpost.com/news/wonk
/wp/2017/08/11/study-one-in-eight-american-adults-are-alcoholics/.

7. S. Carpenter, "Smoking and Depression Perpetuate One Another, Study Indicates,"
Monitor on Psychology 32, no. 7 (June 2001), https://www.apa.org/monitor/jun01
/smokedepress.aspx.

8. Mike Stobbe, "Opioid Epidemic Shares Chilling Similarities with the Past," *Houston Chronicle*, October 30, 2017, https://web.archive.org/web/20171107022338/http://www.chron.com/news/medical/article/Opioid-epidemic-shares-chilling-similarities-with-12313820.php.

9. United States Drug Enforcement Administration, "DEA Issues Nationwide Alert on Fentanyl as Threat to Health and Public Safety," news release, March 18, 2015, https://www.dea.gov/press-releases/2015/03/18/dea-issues-nationwide-alert-fentanyl-threat-health-and-public-safety.

10. Eva Selhub, "Nutritional Psychiatry: Your Brain on Food," *Harvard Health Blog*, November 16, 2015, https://www.health.harvard.edu/blog/nutritional-psychiatry-your-brain-on-food-201511168626.

11. Cecilie Schou Andreassen et al., "The Relationship between Addictive Use of Social Media and Video Games and Symptoms of Psychiatric Disorders: A Large-Scale Cross-Sectional Study," *Psychology of Addictive Behaviors* 30, no. 2 (March 2016): 252–62, http://irep.ntu.ac.uk/id/eprint/27290/7/27290_Kuss.pdf.

12. Shane W. Kraus, Valerie Voon, and Marc N. Potenza, "Neurobiology of Compulsive Sexual Behavior: Emerging Science," *Neuropsychopharmacology* 41, no. 1 (January 2016): 385–86, https://www.researchgate.net/publication/282090679_Neurobiology_of_Compulsive_Sexual_Behavior_Emerging_Science.

13. Jeremiah Weinstock and Carla J. Rash, "Clinical and Research Implications of Gambling Disorder in DSM-5," *Current Addiction Reports* 1, no. 3 (September 2014): 159–65, https://www.ncbi.nlm.nih.gov/pmc/articles/PMC4753073/.

CHAPTER 6: THE THREE DEADLY EMOTIONS

1. "Chronic Stress Puts Your Health at Risk," Mayo Clinic, April 21, 2016, https://www.mayoclinic.org/healthy-lifestyle/stress-management/in-depth/stress/art-20046037.

CHAPTER 7: THE ANTIDOTE FOR TOXIC EMOTIONS

1. "Forgiveness: Your Health Depends on It," Johns Hopkins Medicine, accessed January 7, 2019, https://www.hopkinsmedicine.org/health/healthy_aging/healthy_connections/forgiveness-your-health-depends-on-it.

2. Loren Toussaint and Jon R. Webb, "Theoretical and Empirical Connections between Forgiveness, Mental Health, and Well-Being," in *Handbook of Forgiveness*, ed. Everett L. Worthington Jr. (New York: Routledge, 2005), 355.

CHAPTER 8: STRENGTH THROUGH SOUL CARE

1. Pablo Neruda, *Odes to Common Things* (Boston: Bulfinch Press, 1994), 75.

2. Corporation for National and Community Service, Office of Research and Policy Development, *The Health Benefits of Volunteering: A Review of Recent Research* (Washington, DC, 2007), https://www.nationalservice.gov/pdf/07_0506_hbr.pdf.

3. S. L. Brown et al., "Providing Social Support May Be More Beneficial than Receiving It: Results from a Prospective Study of Mortality," *Psychological Science* 14, no. 4 (July 1, 2003): 320–27, https://www.ncbi.nlm.nih.gov/pubmed/12807404.

4. "Stress Relief from Laughter? It's No Joke," Mayo Clinic, April 21, 2016, https://www.mayoclinic.org/healthy-lifestyle/stress-management/in-depth/stress-relief/art-20044456.

CHAPTER 9: START MOVING AND START IMPROVING

1. James A. Blumenthal, Patrick J. Smith, and Benson M. Hoffman, "Is Exercise a Viable Treatment for Depression?" *ACSM's Health & Fitness Journal* 16, no. 4 (July 2012): 14–21, https://www.ncbi.nlm.nih.gov/pmc/articles/PMC3674785/.

2. George Mammen, quoted at Therese Borchard, "Exercise Not Only Treats, but Prevents Depression," Everyday Health, updated November 7, 2013, https://www.everydayhealth.com/columns/therese-borchard-sanity-break/exercise-not-only-treats-but-prevents-depression/.

3. Samuel B. Harvey et al., "Exercise and the Prevention of Depression: Results of the HUNT Cohort Study," *American Journal of Psychiatry* 175, no. 1 (October 2017): 28–36, https://ajp.psychiatryonline.org/doi/abs/10.1176/appi.ajp.2017.16111223?mobileUi=0&journalCode=ajp.

4. Alpa Patel, quoted at Janet Lee, "How Much Exercise Do You Need to Get Healthier?" *Consumer Reports*, updated February 20, 2019, https://www.consumerreports.org/exercise-fitness/how-much-exercise-do-you-need-to-see-health-benefits/.

5. US Department of Health and Human Services, *Physical Activity Guidelines for Americans, 2nd edition* (Washington, DC: US Department of Health and Human Services, 2018), https://health.gov/paguidelines/second-edition/pdf/Physical_Activity_Guidelines_2nd_edition.pdf.

6. John J. Ratey with Eric Hagerman, *Spark: The Revolutionary New Science of Exercise and the Brain* (New York: Little, Brown, Spring 2008), 129, 136.

7. John Ratey, "The ADHD Exercise Solution," *ADDitude Magazine* (Spring 2008), https://www.additudemag.com/the-adhd-exercise-solution. See also "Green Play Settings Reduce ADHD Symptoms," University of Illinois at Urbana-Champaign, Landscape and Human Health Laboratory, accessed March 7, 2019, http://lhhl.illinois.edu/adhd.htm.

8. Ratey, *Spark*, 140.

9. Michael Bracko, quoted at Dulce Zamora, "Fitness 101: The Absolute Beginner's Guide to Exercise," WebMD, February 12, 2008, https://www.webmd.com/fitness-exercise/features/fitness-beginners-guide#1.

10. "How Does Exercise Help Those with Chronic Insomnia?" National Sleep Foundation, accessed March 7, 2019, https://sleepfoundation.org/ask-the-expert/how-does-exercise-help-those-chronic-insomnia.

11. "Heart Disease Facts," Centers for Disease Control and Prevention, November 28, 2017, https://www.cdc.gov/heartdisease/facts.htm.

12. "Blood Glucose and Exercise," American Diabetes Association, September 25, 2017, http://www.diabetes.org/food-and-fitness/fitness/get-started-safely/blood-glucose-control-and-exercise.html.

13. Marily Oppezzo and Daniel L. Schwartz, "Give Your Ideas Some Legs: The Positive Effect of Walking on Creative Thinking," *Journal of Experimental Psychology: Learning, Memory, and Cognition* 40, no. 4 (July 2014): 1142–52, http://psycnet.apa.org/record/2014-14435-001.

CHAPTER 10: GOOD FOOD = GOOD MOOD

1. Monique Tello, "Diet and Depression," *Harvard Health Blog*, February 22, 2018, https://www.health.harvard.edu/blog/diet-and-depression-2018022213309.

2. Ed Cara, "High-Fat Diet May Convince Us to Overeat by Wreaking Havoc on Our Gut Bacteria," Medical Daily, July 7, 2015, https://www.medicaldaily.com/high-fat -diet-may-convince-us-overeat-wreaking-havoc-our-gut-bacteria-341806.

3. Ye Li et al., "Dietary Patterns and Depression Risk: A Meta-analysis," *Psychiatry Research* 253 (July 2017): 373–82, https://www.ncbi.nlm.nih.gov/pubmed /28431261.

4. Some of this content is adapted from "Depression and Diet," WebMD, updated October 16, 2018, https://www.webmd.com/depression/guide/diet-recovery#1.

5. Colin Poitras, "Even Mild Dehydration Can Alter Mood," *UConn Today*, February 21, 2012, https://today.uconn.edu/2012/02/even-mild-dehydration-can-alter-mood/.

6. This list is adapted from Kathleen M. Zelman, "6 Reasons to Drink Water," WebMD, May 8, 2019, https://www.webmd.com/diet/features/6-reasons-to-drink -water#1.

CHAPTER 11: TIME TO TAKE OUT THE TRASH

1. US Department of Health and Human Services, Washington, DC: *10th Special Report to the U.S. Congress on Alcohol and Health* (US Department of Health and Human Services, June 2000), 134–46, https://pubs.niaaa.nih.gov/publications /10report/10thspecialreport.pdf.

2. Melaina Juntti, "Just 5 Drinks a Week Can Damage Your Brain," *Men's Journal*, accessed March 11, 2019, https://www.mensjournal.com/health-fitness/just-5- drinks-a-week-can-damage-your-brain-w493425/.

3. S. L. Peters et al., "Randomised Clinical Trial: Gluten May Cause Depression in Subjects with Non-Coeliac Gluten Sensitivity—An Exploratory Clinical Study," *Alimentary Pharmacology and Therapeutics* 39, no. 10 (April 1, 2014): 1104–12, https://www.ncbi.nlm.nih.gov/pubmed/24689456.

4. Emily Deans, "Is Gluten Causing Your Depression?" *Psychology Today*, October 4, 2014, https://www.psychologytoday.com/us/blog/evolutionary-psychiatry/201410 /is-gluten-causing-your-depression.

CHAPTER 12: IS YOUR GUT STUCK IN A RUT?

1. Thomas Carlyle, *History of Friedrich the Second, Called Frederick the Great* vol. 1, chap. 6.

2. Gerard Clarke, quoted at Megan Brooks, "'Psychobiotic' May Help Ease Stress, Improve Memory," Medscape, October 20, 2015, https://www.medscape.com/ viewarticle/852944.

3. José F. Siqueira Jr., Ashraf F. Fouad, and Isabela N. Rôças, "Pyrosequencing as a Tool for Better Understanding of Human Microbiomes," *Journal of Oral Microbiology* 4 (January 2012), https://www.tandfonline.com/doi/full/10.3402/jom.v4i0.10743.

4. Franziska Spritzler, "How to Choose the Best Probiotic Supplement," Healthline, January 21, 2017, https://www.healthline.com/nutrition/best-probiotic-supplement.

CHAPTER 13: THE MAGIC OF MICRONUTRIENTS

1. Mark Hyman, *The UltraMind Solution: The Simple Way to Defeat Depression, Overcome Anxiety, and Sharpen Your Mind* (New York: Scribner, 2009), 129.

2. Ibid.

3. Tim Lang, quoted at "Are Fruits/Veggies Really Delivering?" Healthy You Naturally, September 2007, http://www.healthyyounaturally.com/newsletters/0907.htm.
4. The Center served as a test site in the development of the Hope & Possibility line.
5. Baljit K. Khamba et al., "Effectiveness of Vitamin D in the Treatment of Mood Disorders: A Literature Review," *Journal of Orthomolecular Medicine* 26, no. 3 (2011): 127–35, https://www.isom.ca/wp-content/uploads/2013/01/Effectiveness -of-Vitamin-D-in-the-Treatment-of-Mood-Disorders-A-Literature-Review-26.3.pdf.
6. Louis E. Banderet and Harris R. Lieberman, "Treatment with Tyrosine, a Neurotransmitter Precursor, Reduces Environmental Stress in Humans," *Brain Research Bulletin* 22, no. 4 (April 1989): 759–62, https://apps.dtic.mil/dtic/tr /fulltext/u2/a215036.pdf; Alan J. Gelenberg et al., "Tyrosine for Depression," *Journal of Psychiatric Research* 17, no. 2 (1982–83): 175–80, https://www.ncbi .nlm.nih.gov/pubmed/6764934#.
7. The Center served as a test site for the formula in Brain Awakening, a supplement I developed with Redd Remedies.
8. Guosong Liu et al., "Efficacy and Safety of MMFS-01, a Synapse Density Enhancer, for Treating Cognitive Impairment in Older Adults: A Randomized, Double-Blind, Placebo-Controlled Trial," *Journal of Alzheimer's Disease* 49, no. 4 (2016): 971–90, https://www.ncbi.nlm.nih.gov/pmc/articles/PMC4927823/.
9. Caroline Praderio, "9 Horrible Ways That Stress Messes with Your Body—and What You Can Do about It," Insider, August 30, 2017, http://www.thisisinsider.com/health -effects-of-stress-2017-8#stress-could-trigger-depression-9.
10. Vamshi K. Manda et. al., "Modulation of CYPs, P-gp, and PXR by *Eschscholzia californica* (California Poppy) and Its Alkaloids," *Planta Medica* 82, no. 6 (April 2016): 551–58, https://www.ncbi.nlm.nih.gov/pubmed/27054913.
11. Javier Cubero Juanez, "Hops (*Humulus lupulus L.*) and Beer: Benefits on the Sleep," *Journal of Sleep Disorders & Therapy* 1, no. 1 (January 2012), https://www .researchgate.net/publication/269554572_Hops_Humulus_lupulus_L_and_Beer _Benefits_on_the_Sleep.
12. Andrew Scholey et al., "Anti-Stress Effects of Lemon Balm-Containing Foods," *Nutrients* 6, no. 11 (October 2014) 4805–21, https://www.ncbi.nlm.nih.gov/pmc /articles/PMC4245564.
13. B. Abbasi et al., "The Effect of Magnesium Supplementation on Primary Insomnia in Elderly: A Double-Blind Placebo-Controlled Clinical Trial," *Journal of Research in Medical Sciences* 17, no. 12 (December 2012): 1161–69, https://www.ncbi.nlm.nih .gov/pubmed/23853635.

APPENDIX 2: LEAVE NO STONE UNTURNED

1. Hugh MacPherson, quoted at "Acupuncture Boosts Effectiveness of Standard Medical Care for Chronic Pain, Depression," *ScienceDaily*, January 30, 2017, https://www .sciencedaily.com/releases/2017/01/170130083228.htm; Hugh MacPherson et al., "Acupuncture and Counselling for Depression in Primary Care: A Randomised Controlled Trial," *PLOS Medicine* (September 24, 2013), http://journals.plos.org /plosmedicine/article?id=10.1371/journal.pmed.1001518.
2. "Smell of Jasmine 'As Calming as Valium,'" *Telegraph*, July 10, 2010, https://www .telegraph.co.uk/news/science/7881819/Smell-of-jasmine-as-calming-as-valium.html.

3. Dalinda Isabel Sánchez-Vidaña et al., "The Effectiveness of Aromatherapy for Depressive Symptoms: A Systematic Review," *Evidence-Based Complementary and Alternative Medicine*, January 4, 2017, https://www.ncbi.nlm.nih.gov/pmc/articles /PMC5241490.

4. T. Komori et al., "Effects of Citrus Fragrance on Immune Function and Depressive States," *Neuroimmunomodulation* 2, no. 3 (May–June 1995): 174–80, https://www .ncbi.nlm.nih.gov/pubmed/8646568.

5. Jennifer Vande Voort, quoted at Amy Ellis Nutt, "Nasal Spray of Party Drug Shows Promise as Fast-Acting Antidepressant, Researchers Say," *Washington Post*, April 20, 2018, https://www.washingtonpost.com/news/to-your-health/wp/2018/04/20 /nasal-spray-of-party-drug-shows-promise-as-fast-acting-antidepressant-researchers -say/?utm_term=.62124aba2721.

6. Nutt, "Nasal Spray of Party Drug."

7. "Brain Stimulation Therapies," National Institute of Mental Health, June 2016, https://www.nimh.nih.gov/health/topics/brain-stimulation-therapies/brain -stimulation-therapies.shtml.

8. "Transcranial Magnetic Stimulation," Mayo Clinic, November 27, 2018, https:// www.mayoclinic.org/tests-procedures/transcranial-magnetic-stimulation/about/pac -20384625.

9. Kirsten Weir, "Can Magnets Cure Depression?" *Monitor on Psychology* 46, no. 2, (February 2015), https://www.apa.org/monitor/2015/02/magnets.aspx.

10. "Long-Term Benefits of Transcranial Magnetic Stimulation for Depression Supported by New Study," *ScienceDaily*, October 13, 2010, https://www.sciencedaily.com /releases/2010/10/101012114052.htm.

11. Philip G. Janicak and Mehmet E. Dokucu, "Transcranial Magnetic Stimulation for the Treatment of Major Depression," *Neuropsychiatric Disease and Treatment* 2015, no. 11 (June 2015): 1549–60, http://tmshealtheducation.com/wp-content/uploads/2015/12 /Transcranial-magnetic-stimulation-for-the-treatment-of-major-depression.pdf.

12. Weir, "Can Magnets Cure Depression?"

APPENDIX 3: WHOLE HEALTH MATTERS

1. Dima Mazen Qato, Katharine Ozenberger, and Mark Olfson, "Prevalence of Prescription Medications with Depression as a Potential Adverse Effect among Adults in the United States," *Journal of the American Medical Association* 319, no. 22 (June 12, 2018): 2289–98, https://jamanetwork.com/journals/jama/article-abstract/2684607.

2. Fuschia M. Sirois, Michelle L. Melia-Gordon, Timothy A. Pychyl, "'I'll Look After My Health, Later': An Investigation of Procrastination and Health," *Personality and Individual Differences* 35, no. 5 (October 2003): 1167–84, https://www .sciencedirect.com/science/article/pii/S0191886902003264; Fuschia M. Sirois, Wendelien van Eerde, and Maria Ioanna Argiropoulou, "Is Procrastination Related to Sleep Quality? Testing an Application of the Procrastination–Health Model," *Cogent Psychology* 2, no. 1 (2015), https://www.tandfonline.com/doi/full/10.1080 /23311908.2015.1074776.

3. Barrett Wissman, "An Accountability Partner Makes You Vastly More Likely to Succeed," *Entrepreneur*, March 20, 2018, https://www.entrepreneur.com/article /310062.

About the Authors

Mental health expert **Dr. Gregory Jantz** pioneered whole-person, holistic care. Now recognized as one of the leaders in holistic treatment, Dr. Jantz continues to identify more effective, cutting-edge forms of treatment for people struggling with eating disorders, depression, anxiety, and trauma. He is the founder of The Center: A Place of Hope, which was voted one of the top 10 facilities in the United States for the treatment of depression.

Dr. Jantz is a bestselling author of more than 37 books. He is a go-to media source for a range of behavioral-based afflictions, including drug and alcohol addictions. Dr. Jantz has appeared on CNN, FOX, ABC, and CBS and has been interviewed for the *New York Post*, Associated Press, *Family Circle*, and *Woman's Day*. He is also a regular contributor to the *Thrive Global* and *Psychology Today* blogs. Visit www.aplaceofhope.com and www.drgregoryjantz.com.

Keith Wall, a twenty-five-year publishing veteran, is an award-winning author, magazine editor, radio scriptwriter, and online columnist. He currently writes full time in collaboration with several bestselling authors. Keith lives in a mountaintop cabin near Manitou Springs, Colorado.

Discover new hope for lasting relief!

GREGORY L. JANTZ, PhD

The Personalized Approach that Offers New Hope for Lasting Relief

Healing Depression for Life

Find a new way forward for overcoming your feelings of hopelessness and uncovering lasting peace with this new book from Dr. Gregory Jantz.

GREGORY L. JANTZ, PhD

The 12-Week Journey to Lifelong Wellness

Healing Depression for Life WORKBOOK

A companion resource to the book *Healing Depression for Life* that will bring you closer to healing and wholeness.

GREGORY L. JANTZ, PhD

Soul Care

Prayers, Scriptures, and Spiritual Practices for When You Need Hope the Most

A HEALING DEPRESSION FOR LIFE RESOURCE

A collection of inspirational quotes, Scriptures, and prayers to help you lead a healthy, faith-filled life.

www.tyndale.com

CP1486

THE CENTER
A PLACE OF HOPE

Voted a Top 10 Facility for the Treatment of Depression in the United States

Hope and Healing for the **Whole You**

For over 30 years, **The Center • A Place of HOPE** has been helping people change their lives for good. Our treatment programs are unique and life changing. We look at the "whole you", not just the parts you want us to see. We dig deeper, walking alongside you with customized care and treatment plans aimed at healing you emotionally, physically, and spiritually.

Are you suffering from depression, addictions, anger, eating disorders, PTSD, emotional and sexual abuse, family and marital problems, or spiritual burnout? We understand your pain and, more importantly, we understand recovery. We are ready to work with you, to help you rediscover the real you and return balance, peace and happiness to your life again.

For more information about any of our programs including current program rates, please contact us for a free initial consultation.

Call: 1.888.771.5166

email: info@aplaceofhope.com

Learn more about leading edge options for treating Depression and take our online Depression questionnaire at:

www.aplaceofhope.com

A Vision of **HOPE and HEALING** for the Whole-Person

Pioneering whole-person care and best-selling author of over 38 books, **Dr. Gregory Jantz** has dedicated his life's work to developing ways to help people change their lives for good.

Bringing together a team of world class professionals to address the medical, physical, psychological, emotional, and spiritual considerations involved in recovery through his whole-person approach, Dr. Jantz founded **The Center • A Place of HOPE** to help people transform their lives.

For speaking engagements and media inquiries, please contact:
Beth Chapman • bethc@aplaceofhope.com • 1.800.492.3910

Visit Dr. Jantz online: www.drgregoryjantz.com

CHANGING LIVES FOR GOOD

CP1488